LUTHERAN
A
looks at...

EPISCOPALIANS

James F. Pope

Northwestern Publishing House
Milwaukee, Wisconsin

Art Director: Karen Knutson
Designer: Pamela Dunn

All Scripture quotations, unless otherwise indicated, are taken from the HOLY BIBLE, NEW INTERNATIONAL VERSION®. NIV®. Copyright © 1973, 1978, 1984 by International Bible Society. Used by permission of Zondervan. All rights reserved.

The "NIV" and "New International Version" trademarks are registered in the United States Patent and Trademark Office by International Bible Society. Use of either trademark requires the permission of International Bible Society.

Library of Congress Control Number: 2007940162
Northwestern Publishing House
1250 N. 113th St., Milwaukee, WI 53226-3284
www.nph.net
© 2008 by Northwestern Publishing House
Published 2008
Printed in the United States of America
ISBN 978-0-8100-2058-0

CONTENTS

Introduction. iv

1 Episcopal Church Identity and History. 1

2 Episcopal Church Organization 8

3 Anglican Approach to Worship
and Holy Scripture 18

4 Anglican Approach to Theology:
Salvation and the Sacraments 30

5 The Episcopal Church and the
Issues of Homosexuality and Abortion. 51

6 The Episcopal Church and Uniformity 67

7 The Episcopal Church and Other Churches 74

8 Interviews with an Episcopalian Bishop,
a Priest, and the Presiding Bishop 82

9 Meeting Individual Episcopalians. 93

Conclusion 100

Endnotes. 104

INTRODUCTION

Why write a book about Episcopalians and have a Lutheran do it? There are good answers to both parts of that question.

In recent years, the Episcopal Church has been in the headlines. In 1997 the Evangelical Lutheran Church in America and the Episcopal Church of the United States adopted a "full Communion agreement." The agreement said that each recognized the other church as a true church. While they remained independent churches, they could now cooperate in joint ministries, join in worship and Communion, and allow the clergy from one church to serve in the other. That agreement became official in January 2001 and was celebrated in a joint worship service in the National Cathedral in Washington, DC, which is an Episcopal Church.

More recently, in 2003 the Episcopal Church created headlines by ratifying the consecration of an openly gay bishop, Rev. V. Gene Robinson, who had been elected bishop of the New Hampshire diocese. Robinson's election as bishop sparked controversy inside and outside the Episcopal Church.

Perhaps you are acquainted with the Episcopal Church because of its image. Maybe it's the familiar red doors of the churches, inviting people to find safety and refuge inside. Maybe it's the familiar street sign that says "The Episcopal Church welcomes you" and then points in the direction of the local parish. Whatever the reason, the Episcopal Church is no stranger to Americans. It has been part of the American scene since the days of our Founding Fathers, and the roots of the church go back even farther than that.

But why have a Lutheran do the writing? The answer is partly that a Lutheran pastor like me does not view the

Episcopal Church as something foreign or unknown. When I look at the history of the Episcopal Church and the wider Anglican community to which it belongs, I am taken back to Reformation history. The Lutheran church and the Episcopal Church's parent body, the Church of England, can both trace their beginnings to the Protestant Reformation.

In addition, when I look at the Anglican liturgy, I recognize some Lutheran liturgical forms. But don't be misled by that. The Lutheran church and the Anglican Church sharing common worship forms does not mean they share the same beliefs in all matters. Worship forms are one thing; the content of worship forms is quite another.

This book is intended to give you an overview of the history and beliefs of the Episcopal Church. Its purpose is not to explain what the average member of the Episcopal Church believes. As will be demonstrated, that would be a difficult, if not impossible, task. I say that because the Episcopal Church wholeheartedly encourages independent thought. The Episcopal Church is not a confessional church like the Lutheran church, having confessions that bind and unite the faith of its members. While the Episcopal Church acknowledges confessional statements that are of Episcopalian or Anglican origin, it thinks of these statements more as historical documents than as confessions that bind the faith of its members. The confessions of the Episcopal Church today are the Apostles' and Nicene Creeds. Because the creeds describe Christian doctrine in general terms, the door is open for Episcopalians to view matters of faith in various ways. Because of that, there are no "average members." Rather, there are members who agree in some matters of belief, disagree in others, and find common ground in their worship life and heritage.

From the outset, I want to make it clear why the Episcopal Church is considered a Christian church. That is because it bears the marks of the church: it proclaims the gospel and administers the sacraments. Jesus Christ is held up as Savior. True, some

Episcopal Church clergy members say things that depart from historic Christian beliefs. But any church body can have clergy and laity that go beyond what the church officially professes.

Perhaps at this point a word about confessional Lutherans is in order. By confessional Lutherans I mean those who understand the Christian faith as explained in the Lutheran Confessions: the three ecumenical creeds, the Augsburg Confession, the Apology to the Augsburg Confession, the Smalcald Articles, Luther's Small and Large Catechisms, and the Formula of Concord. Confessional Lutherans subscribe to what the confessions uphold and what they condemn. In other words, confessional Lutherans believe there are *boundaries* to Christian faith and practice; people cannot believe or do whatever they want and still call themselves Lutherans. It is unfortunate, but many Lutheran church bodies that were confessional in the past have jettisoned the confessions to keep up with modern thought and to avoid the stigma of being politically incorrect. References in this book to confessional Lutheranism refer to Lutherans and Lutheran churches that still look to the Lutheran Confessions as a correct exposition of God's Word, and then follow the confessions in their beliefs and practices.

Throughout this book, I will make mention of a survey of Episcopal Church clergy. This was an electronic survey that I initiated in the summer of 2004 to prepare for writing this book. I am indebted to the many Episcopal clergy throughout the country who responded to the survey and explained their beliefs. I am also indebted to the clergy and laity of the Episcopal Church who gave me time for personal conversation. I am especially grateful to Bishop James L. Jelinek of the Minnesota Diocese of the Episcopal Church and Rev. Paul Rider of St. John Episcopal Church in Mankato, Minnesota, for the interviews they granted me, and to members of St. John Episcopal Church for participating in a focus group. Finally, I am grateful to Rev. Katharine Jefferts Schori, the Presiding Bishop of the Episcopal Church, for taking part in an e-mail interview. I have used the information gathered from this research to paint what I hope is an accurate picture of the contemporary Episcopal Church.

1 EPISCOPAL CHURCH
Identity and History

Preview: The Episcopal Church has a membership of 2.3 million people and is part of the worldwide Anglican Communion. While the Episcopal Church did not officially organize until the late 18th century, its roots can be traced back to the 16th century.

Membership

Do you know any Episcopalians? Even if you don't know an Episcopalian personally, you know some of them from a distance. You may recognize the following Episcopalians from the entertainment world: Vincent Price, Ethel Merman, Robin Williams, Jerry Garcia, Judy Collins, Duke Ellington, Nat King Cole, Natalie Cole, and Leslie Uggams. In the sports world, Jerry Glanville and Sammy Sosa are identified as Episcopalians.

A sizable number of United States presidents have had ties to the Episcopal Church: George Washington, James Madison, James Monroe, William Henry Harrison, John Tyler, Zachary Taylor, Franklin Pierce, Chester A. Arthur, Franklin D. Roosevelt, Gerald R. Ford, and George H. W. Bush.

The Episcopal Church can claim two well-known US Supreme Court justices: Sandra Day O'Connor and Thurgood Marshall.

Other notable Episcopalians are former US Secretary of State Colin Powell, former astronaut Buzz Aldrin, pollster George Gallup, financier J. P. Morgan, and anthropologist Margaret Mead.[1]

Episcopalians have a strong presence in the United States Senate. In 2007 Episcopalians comprised 10 percent of the

Senate: Evan Bayh (D-Indiana), Lincoln Chafee (R-Rhode Island), Saxby Chambliss (R-Georgia), Chuck Hagel (R-Nebraska), Blanche Lincoln (D-Arkansas), Bill Nelson (D-Florida), Ted Stevens (R-Alaska), Kay Bailey Hutchison (R-Texas), John McCain (R-Arizona), and John Warner (R-Virginia).[2]

That means that a relatively small church body has a somewhat loud voice in Washington, DC. Episcopalians in the United States House of Representatives in 2007 numbered 27 out of a denomination that comprises 1.7 percent of the total United States population.[3] (In comparison, there were 18 Lutherans in the 110th Congress, coming from Lutheran church bodies in the United States that comprise about 4.6 percent of the US population.[4])

As of 2006, there were about 2.3 million Episcopalians. You can find Episcopalians in more than 7,200 parishes throughout the United States. Those parishes, in turn, are grouped into one hundred domestic dioceses. (There are also ten dioceses outside the United States.) The size of the Episcopal Church is comparable to The Lutheran Church—Missouri Synod, which in 2005 numbered 2.5 million members in 6,144 congregations. However, these two churches differ greatly in the number of their clergy. The Episcopal Church lists over 17,000 as clergy (28 percent of whom are female), while The Lutheran Church—Missouri Synod has a clergy list of about 9,030.

The Anglican Communion

The Episcopal Church belongs to the Anglican Communion, named after the Church of England. The Anglican Communion has over 80 million people who belong to about 40 different church bodies and live in more than 160 countries throughout the world. Member churches of the Anglican Communion include the Anglican Church of Canada, the Church of Ireland, La Iglesia Anglicana de México, the Church of Pakistan (United), and the Church of the Province of West Africa, among others. The Anglican Communion is a worldwide group of people joined together by common traditions, a rich heritage, and worship forms.

How old is the Episcopal Church, and how did it start?

The history and heritage of the Episcopal Church began in England. Christianity has a long history in England and the British Isles. One tradition says that Simon the Zealot, 1 of Jesus' 12 disciples, traveled to England to proclaim the gospel. Another tradition says that the apostle Paul brought the gospel to England. But these stories cannot be proved.

The actual historical record of Christianity in England goes back to the late 2nd century A.D. Christians in England, Ireland, and Scotland had formed the Celtic church. While these Christians shared common beliefs with Christians on the European mainland, they had their own unique rituals, including a separate church calendar.

Roman Church in England

In 596 Pope Gregory I sent a missionary by the name of Augustine to England. (He is not to be confused with the earlier church theologian, Augustine of Hippo.) Mission work in England blossomed, and the Roman Church established a strong foothold there. As the Roman Church in England grew, so did tensions between it and the old Celtic church. Those tensions even involved the royal family in England, some of whom aligned themselves with the Roman Church and others with the Celtic church. Such a situation could not continue. But which church would prevail? A meeting of the minds from both church and state would determine the outcome.

The Synod of Whitby

In 664 King Oswy held court at a monastery in Whitby in order to decide the issue. After questioning both the Roman and the Celtic representatives, he was swayed by the Roman Catholic Church's interpretation of Matthew 16:17-19, which the Roman Church interprets to be the institution of the papacy. He ruled that Roman Christianity be preferred over Celtic Christianity. Thus England became subject to Rome in its theology and church calendar. And what a loyal subject it was for so many years. One author noted: "Among all the Teutonic tribes, the English became the most devoted subjects of the Pope. They sent more pilgrims to Rome and more money into the papal treasury than any other nation."[5] England's cordial association with Rome continued for hundreds of years. But in the 16th century that relationship would be strained and finally severed.

The Reformation

King Henry VIII of England was 26 years old when Martin Luther nailed his Ninety-five Theses to the door of the Castle Church in Wittenberg. While the sound of Luther's hammer did not reach Henry's ears, the content of Luther's writings did. In the early part of his reign, Henry was a loyal supporter of Rome. In fact, as Luther was publicly exposing Rome's false teachings, Henry attacked Luther and defended Rome. Rome appreciated Henry's defense so much that it honored him with the title "Defender of the Faith."

But the mutual admiration between Henry and Rome soon came to an end. The issue was Henry's marital life (he eventually had six wives). Henry's first marriage, to Catherine of Aragon, did not produce the son he desperately needed to keep his dynasty active. Dissatisfaction with Catherine led Henry to become interested in another woman, Anne Boleyn. Henry asked Pope Clement VII to annul his marriage with Catherine. This was not an unusual request, since popes, for a fee, had annulled marriages in the past. When Henry sensed that the pope was dragging his feet on the issue, he bypassed Rome and turned to the church officials in England for help. Thomas Cranmer, the Archbishop of Canterbury, gave Henry the permission he wanted. Cranmer ruled that Henry's marriage to Catherine was "null and absolutely void."

A year later, in 1534, at Henry's urging the English Parliament passed the Act of Supremacy. That act ended papal authority in England and established Henry as the head of the Christian church in England. The Church of England, the parent church of the Episcopalians, formally emerged as an independent Christian church.

Colonization leads to separation

For two centuries, despite violent political struggles in England, the Church of England remained intact. Colonization in North America did not immediately lead to a break in the Anglican church, but when British colonists began resisting the British monarch, it was almost inevitable that Anglican church members in the colonies organize into a new church body.

During the Revolutionary War, many Church of England clergy and laity living in the American colonies found themselves caught between a rock and a hard place. On the one hand, they were rebelling against the mother country, England; and on the other hand, they were using the liturgies and prayers of the 1662 *Book of Common Prayer,* whose forms led them to pray for the royal family of England and for the Parliament. Something had to give.

These colonists sought to remain Anglican but independent of the Church of England. The most difficult problem was how to secure a bishop for the church in the New World. As the next chapter will point out, the apostolic succession of bishops figures prominently in the structure and theology of the Anglican Church. British colonists in North America realized that the Church of England would not appoint a dissenter to the British crown to lead their new church.

However, the British colonists were a resourceful group. They approached officials of the Church of England in Scotland, which had problems of its own with the Anglicans. The Scottish officials readily honored the colonists' request and consecrated Samuel Seabury as the first American bishop of the Anglican Church. The year was 1784. In the following year, the first general convention of the Protestant Episcopal Church in the United States (the official name of the church) took place. The year after that, three more American bishops were consecrated and, more important, recognized by the Church of England. These were the humble beginnings of the Episcopal Church.

The official seal and flag of the Episcopal Church illustrate the main events of the church's history. One parish explains the flag this way: "It is red, white and blue . . . the colors of both the US and England. The red Cross of St. George on a white field symbolizes the Church of England. The blue field in the upper left corner represents the Episcopal Church of the USA. It features a Cross of St. Andrew, in recognition of the fact that the first American bishop was consecrated in Scotland. This cross is made up of nine crosslets, which represent the nine dioceses that met in Philadelphia in 1789 to form the Protestant Episcopal Church of the USA."[6]

This is the history of the Episcopal Church. But what would this new church be like? Would it be an American version of the Church of England, or would it be a radically different group?

Review: The Episcopal Church is similar in size to The Lutheran Church—Missouri Synod. The Episcopal Church belongs to the Anglican Communion, a worldwide fellowship of some 80 million people.

The Church of England came into existence in the 16th century when King Henry VIII was seeking to annul his marriage to Catherine of Aragon. Shortly after Henry received his annulment from the Archbishop of Canterbury, the English Parliament declared that the Christian church in England would be free from the influence of the Roman Catholic Church.

The formation of the Episcopal Church came about two centuries later when American colonists who were affiliated with the Church of England sought independence from England and its rule. The colonists desired to retain the worship, theology, and heritage of the Church of England, so they established an American version of the Church of England—the Episcopal Church.

2 EPISCOPAL CHURCH *Organization*

Preview: The Episcopal Church has three orders of ordained ministers: bishops, priests, and deacons. There is an internal and external organizational structure to guide the church in its life as an independent church body and as a member of the worldwide Anglican Communion.

When the Episcopal Church formally organized in Philadelphia, Pennsylvania, in October 1789, the church's constitution called for a two-chamber structure: the House of Bishops and the House of Deputies. Interestingly enough, this structure resembled the colonists' newly formed legislative branch of government: the Senate and the House of Representatives. Which, in turn, were similar to what the colonists had known in England with the House of Lords and the House of Commons.

The Protestant Episcopal Church in the United States

You will often see the church referred to by its abbreviation: ECUSA (The Episcopal Church in the United States). But in 1789 the church was officially named the Protestant Episcopal Church in the United States. The word *Protestant* in the church's title is significant. While there may be some similarities to the Roman Catholic Church in worship forms and some organizational structures, Episcopalians want it known that they are not Roman Catholics. The word *Protestant* makes it clear that the Episcopal Church does not see eye to eye with the Roman Catholic Church.

The word *Episcopal* in the church's title is also significant. Although the Episcopal Church has worship forms and beliefs that parallel some Protestant churches, Episcopalians want it known that they are not strictly Protestants either. They are Episcopalians. They belong to the Protestant Episcopal Church in the United States.

Bishops, priests, and deacons

Episcopal comes from the Greek word *episkopos*. This is the word "overseer" in 1 Timothy 3:1: "Here is a trustworthy saying: If anyone sets his heart on being an overseer, he desires a noble task." Another name for an overseer of souls in a congregation is pastor. The King James Version translated *episkopos* in 1 Timothy 3:1 as "bishop." Both "overseer" and "bishop" are legitimate translations of the word *episkopos*.

As the early Christian church developed, the word *bishop* came to be used in two ways. Some bishops served in local congregations while others served in a supervisory capacity over larger geographical areas. The history of the early Christian church reveals the strife that developed among the more powerful bishops, until finally the bishop of Rome claimed prominence over the other bishops.

The Episcopal Church views the office of bishop as an important part of its organizational structure and religious heritage. Bishops, priests, and deacons are the three orders that make up its ordained ministry.

Bishops

"Members of the Episcopal Church, if asked, would probably say they value bishops most for two roles: their symbolic role in uniting the church historically with the apostles and their pastoral leadership in the diocese."[7] That comment from an Episcopalian publication underscores the Episcopalian belief in the apostolic succession of bishops. Apostolic succession is the belief that bishops who serve today are part of a long, unbroken line that stretches back to the early days of the New Testament church. Going back to King Henry VIII and the split from Rome,

Episcopalians believe that the Episcopal Church, not the Roman Catholic Church, continues the line of bishops that were established in the early centuries of the Christian church.

The Book of Common Prayer states:

The ministry of a bishop is to represent Christ and his Church, particularly as apostle, chief priest, and pastor of a diocese; to guard the faith, unity, and discipline of the whole Church; to proclaim the Word of God; to act in Christ's name for the reconciliation of the world and the building up of the Church; and to ordain others to continue Christ's ministry.[8]

Bishops are responsible for the general oversight of their dioceses. (A diocese is a geographical area of the church.) In that respect, they are like district presidents in some Lutheran church bodies. One Lutheran church body, the Evangelical Lutheran Church in America (ELCA), still uses the title of bishop in their hierarchical structure. But because the Episcopal Church does not recognize the bishops of ELCA as part of the apostolic succession, a special exception had to be made in order for the two churches to enter into full communion. Chapter 7 will explain in greater detail the relationship between those two churches.

There are some notable differences between Episcopal Church bishops and Lutheran district presidents. When it comes to the ordination of a priest or deacon in the Episcopal Church, it is a bishop who ordains that person into the ministry. In Lutheran churches, the authority to ordain is not limited to district presidents. Also, youth and adult confirmations in the diocese must be performed by the bishop.

In addition to these responsibilities, bishops help the congregations in their dioceses fill priest or deacon vacancies. Bishops are required to regularly visit the congregations in their dioceses. Unlike the Roman Catholic Church, bishops in the Episcopal Church can be married and they can be female. As of 2002, 11 of the 222 bishops were women.[9]

Priests

The second order of ordained ministers in the Episcopal Church are the priests. Again, unlike the Roman Catholic Church, priests in the Episcopal Church can be married and they can be female. The Episcopal Church first voted to allow women to enter the priesthood in 1976. Currently, approximately 14 percent of the clergy in the Episcopal Church are women.

The Book of Common Prayer states that "the ministry of a priest is to represent Christ and his Church, particularly as pastor to the people; to share with the bishop in overseeing the Church; to proclaim the Gospel; to administer the sacraments; and to bless and declare pardon in the name of God."[10] Priests have responsibilities similar to Lutheran parish pastors. A priest's title may vary according to the nature of the parish. In a self-supporting, established parish, the priest is called a *rector*. In a mission-supported parish, the priest is a *vicar*, which means "substitute," because in that parish the priest represents the bishop.

How a person trains for the priesthood in the Episcopal Church varies. There are 11 Episcopal seminaries in the United States that offer training for the priesthood. However, not every person who wants to become a priest in the Episcopal Church is required to attend one of those seminaries, or any seminary for that matter. It is possible for a person to be trained in his parish and then serve that parish as its priest.

Deacons

Deacons are the third order of ordained ministers in the Episcopal Church. As with the two previous orders, deacons can be married and can be female (deaconesses). In this order, females form the majority. *The Book of Common Prayer* states that "the ministry of a deacon is to represent Christ and his Church, particularly as a servant of those in need; and to assist bishops and priests in the proclamation of the Gospel and the administration of the sacraments."[11] Beyond assisting the priests during worship services, "it is also a special responsibility of deacons to minister in Christ's name to the poor, the sick, the suffering, and the helpless."[12] Some Lutherans might notice similarities between deacons in the Episcopal Church and staff ministers in their own congregations. A typical deacon(ness) in the Episcopal Church serves on a part-time basis and also has secular employment.

Parish makeup

Episcopal parishes want to involve their lay members. In fact, *The Book of Common Prayer* explains that "the ministers of the Church are lay persons, bishops, priests, and deacons."[13] One Episcopal Church priest told me how he thought it was significant that the laity were mentioned first in that listing.

One of the ways laypeople are involved in the leadership of local parishes is through the *vestry*. Vestries are similar to church councils in Lutheran congregations. The vestry consists of men and women elected by their parish to positions of leadership. Leading the vestry is the senior warden. That position is similar to congregational chairmen in Lutheran congregations. The primary responsibilities of the vestry are to manage the parish finances and see to it that the church is kept in good repair. The vestry tries to take care of the parish's business matters so that the ordained ministers can focus on the work of their calling.

Wider organization

Each Episcopal parish is located in a diocese, which is a cluster of parishes in a certain geographical area, presided over by a bishop. A group of dioceses, in turn, form a province. There are nine provinces in the Episcopal Church. Eight of the provinces are domestic, while one is international. For example, Province 1 consists of the dioceses of Connecticut, Maine, Massachusetts, New Hampshire, Rhode Island, Vermont, and Western Massachusetts. Province 9, the international province, is made up of the dioceses of Colombia, the Dominican Republic, Ecuador, Honduras, Puerto Rico, and Venezuela. Each province elects its own president. Each province also has a House of Bishops, made up of active and retired bishops from that province; and a House of Deputies, a group representing the priests, deacons, and laypeople in the province. At the diocesan and provincial levels, conventions consisting of clergy and laity plan and guide the work of the church.

A separate House of Bishops and a House of Deputies guide the national church. The leader of the national church is the Presiding Bishop. That position is comparable to the position of synod president in Lutheran churches. The current Presiding Bishop is Rev. Katharine Jefferts Schori. She was elected to a nine-year term at the church's General Convention in 2006.

Anglican organization

The structure of the Episcopal Church is not entirely unlike that of other churches. In addition to the internal structure of the Protestant Episcopal Church in the USA as described previously, there is also an external structure that guides the church as a member of the Anglican Communion. This external structure is somewhat complex. The Episcopal Church is one of 38 national church bodies that belong to the Anglican Communion. (The Episcopal Church's association within the Anglican Communion can be seen on the church's official Web site at www.ecusa.anglican.org.) It may come as a surprise, but there is no legislative body that supervises the doctrine and practice of all the member churches of the Anglican Communion. That autonomy stems from the Anglican spirit, but such independence can cause difficulty, as the recent controversies over homosexuality and same-sex marriages illustrate.

"The Anglican Communion is not a federation, nor in the strict sense a confessional family. It is held together more by common loyalties than by organizational structures."[14] The churches of the Anglican Communion acknowledge four "instruments of unity" that are to encourage and invite cooperation within the church. The instruments of unity are the Archbishop of Canterbury, the Lambeth Conference, the Anglican Consultative Council, and the Primates' Meeting. These instruments of unity encourage and invite cooperation but lack authority to intervene when churches do not cooperate with one another.

The Archbishop of Canterbury

Even before the Church of England distanced itself from Rome in the days of King Henry VIII, the Archbishop of Canterbury held a position of influence in the church. While the Archbishop of Canterbury remains a very influential person in the Church of England today, his relationship to other churches in the Anglican Communion, such as the Episcopal Church, is less prescriptive and more advisory. "The role of the Archbishop of Canterbury, as the historic first bishop in the Church of England and thus in Anglicanism, has the power of recognition and invitation. What does that mean? Technically speaking, to be an Anglican means to be 'in communion' with the See of Canterbury, or in other words: recognized with the Archbishop of Canterbury. If you are not 'in communion' with Canterbury then you would have a difficult time saying that you are an Anglican."[15] As an instrument of unity, the Archbishop of Canterbury is the symbolic head of the Anglican Communion. Because he lacks authority to impose his will on Episcopalians or on any other members of the Anglican Communion, he is not to be considered as the counterpart to the Roman Catholic pontiff.

The Lambeth Conference

In 1867 bishops of the Anglican Communion met at Lambeth Palace, the residence of the Archbishop of Canterbury, to respond to controversies within the Communion over creation and evolution. Because of the meeting's location, the gathering became known as the Lambeth Conference. The conference addressed the controversies with resolutions and statements but lacked the authority to do anything else. Still, the bishops found it worthwhile to gather together and discuss theological matters. The result of that first conference is that there has been a gathering of bishops of the Anglican Communion approximately every ten years since 1867, except during wartime. The last conference was held in 1998.

While the conference is advisory in nature, "Its deliberations command considerable moral authority. From time to time it has made significant pronouncements."[16] "The Lambeth Conference has no legal authority over any one church in the Anglican Communion, but reports and resolutions passed by the Bishops do have power since they represent the mind of the bishops gathered together."[17]

The Anglican Consultative Council

The third instrument of unity for the Anglican Communion is the Anglican Consultative Council. "The Anglican Consultative Council (ACC) is the most comprehensive gathering of the Anglican Communion, representing the voice of the inner life of the provinces."[18] The Council meets "every 3 years or so."[19] It is a comprehensive gathering because it includes representatives from the three orders of ordained ministers and also lay members. In fact, it is the only instrument of unity that involves laypeople.

There is something else significant about the ACC. "One key difference between the ACC and the Lambeth Conference and Primates' Meeting is that the ACC is the only incorporated body of the Anglican Communion and as such has legal status as a charity and fiscal entity for the Communion."[20] However, in spite of that difference, the Anglican Consultative Council, like the other instruments of unity, is only advisory in nature.

The Primates' Meeting

The fourth instrument of unity is the Primates' Meeting. This group consists of the top leaders of the 38 member churches that constitute the Anglican Communion. For example, one of the members of this instrument of unity is the Presiding Bishop of the Episcopal Church. The Primates' Meeting is an annual event. However, the members of this group do not have authority beyond the individual churches they represent. As a recent document from the Anglican Communion noted, "Like the other Instruments of Unity . . . the Primates' Meeting has refused to acknowledge anything more than a consultative and advisory authority."[21]

One recent piece of "advice" that came out of the Primates' Meeting in February 2005 was that "the Episcopal Church (USA) and the Anglican Church of Canada voluntarily withdraw their members from the Anglican Consultative Council for the period leading up to the next Lambeth Conference."[22] That action came about in the context of the Anglican Communion's debate over homosexuality and same-sex marriages.

The Anglican Communion has instruments in place to promote and encourage unity, but those instruments lack the authority to intervene when a member church threatens the unity. And so, as an Anglican Communion document observed: "We have a 'Council' which is 'consultative', a 'Conference' which meets once a decade, a 'Meeting' which has no prescribed timetable, and an 'Archbishop'."[23] This seemingly unworkable system has succeeded in keeping the Anglican Communion together for quite some time, but there are voices within the Communion that want their governing instruments to have authority of some kind to maintain the unity.

The Lambeth Commission on Communion is one of those voices. This commission is a special committee of Anglicans appointed by the Archbishop of Canterbury to study the ramifications of the consecration of an Episcopal gay bishop and the same-sex marriage rites developed by a province in the Anglican Church of Canada. In October 2004, the commission made several recommendations, including the drafting of the Anglican Covenant, a document to which all the churches of the Anglican Communion would subscribe their allegiance, and the promoting of the Archbishop of Canterbury as the focal point of unity. Time will tell what the Anglican Communion does with the commission's recommendations.

One would be surprised, however, if the Anglican Covenant were adopted because that would restrict the faith and practice of Anglicans and lead them in the direction of becoming a confessional church body. And Anglicans are not used to that.

Perhaps you are wondering how unity is maintained in the Anglican Communion without a governing body. Part of the answer lies in a book, as we shall see in the next chapter.

Review: Bishops, priests, and deacons form the three orders of ordained ministers in the Episcopal Church. Parishes are grouped together in dioceses and are under the supervision of bishops. The church governs itself by means of conventions in the dioceses and a General Convention at the national level. Four "instruments of unity" are in place to urge cooperation between the Episcopal Church and other churches of the Anglican Communion. They are the Archbishop of Canterbury, the Lambeth Conference, the Anglican Consultative Council, and the Primates' Meeting.

3 ANGLICAN APPROACH
TO WORSHIP AND
Holy Scripture

Preview: Like the Lutheran church, the Episcopal Church has a rich liturgical heritage. The Book of Common Prayer is the worship and devotional book that most identify with the Episcopal Church, and it serves as a unifying factor among its members. The Episcopal Church views reason and tradition, in addition to Scripture, as sources of authority in their faith and life. That approach allows a diversity of thought within the church.

A Lutheran who visits an Episcopal parish where the traditional liturgy is being used will probably be impressed by its majesty and formality. While contemporary worship is also making inroads into Episcopalian parishes, traditional worship is still the dominant style. A Lutheran who visits an Episcopal parish that uses either the traditional or a contemporary worship will most likely find up to three books in the pew racks: a hymnal, a Bible, and *The Book of Common Prayer*. *The Book of Common Prayer* will most certainly be there. That book has been at the forefront of Anglican worship for over 450 years and still has a profound influence in the Episcopal Church. One Episcopalian author, who recently wrote an introduction to his church, made this comment: "Other churches may find their unity in an organizational system or a set of beliefs, but Episcopalians find their unity first of all in worship using *The Book of Common Prayer*."[24]

But where did *The Book of Common Prayer* originate? How did it come into being? The answers take us first to England, then to Germany, and finally back to England.

Lutheran influence

At a focus group I conducted in preparation for writing this book, an elderly Episcopalian gentleman related his first experience in attending a Lutheran worship service. When the service was over, he said to the Lutheran friend with whom he had attended: "You Lutherans stole your whole liturgy from us!" History, however, does not support that accusation. In fact, the historical record reveals the great influence that Lutheran liturgical practices had on the Church of England during its infancy.

When the Church of England formed during the reign of King Henry VIII, it needed worship forms that reflected its new identity. The person who spearheaded the effort to compile those worship forms was Thomas Cranmer, the Archbishop of Canterbury. Cranmer was a contemporary of Martin Luther. While those two men never met, Luther's ideas influenced Cranmer. Cranmer had several meetings with Luther's colleague Philip Melanchthon, and he had contacts with other Lutherans as well. While on royal assignment in Germany to work out an agreement with Lutherans (an agreement that never materialized), Cranmer wound up living in the home of a prominent German Lutheran pastor for about a year. (He eventually married the pastor's niece.) It so happened that during his stay in the Lutheran parsonage, the local Lutherans were developing a liturgy. Cranmer observed much of the process, brought back many liturgical ideas to England, and incorporated them in what became known as *The Book of Common Prayer.* A noted historian of church liturgics observed that "the orders for baptism, confirmation, marriage, and burial reveal extensive indebtedness to Lutheran sources."[25] In addition, Cranmer translated a German Lutheran catechism into English. Indeed, "the influences of German church orders on the Prayer Book are obvious."[26]

The Book of Common Prayer was first published in 1549, three years after Luther's death. The book has had several major revisions. However, revisions are not made lightly. In England, a revision of *The Book of Common Prayer* requires an act of Parliament. For the Episcopal Church in the USA, a revision requires the consent of the General Convention. *The Book of Common Prayer* currently in use in the Episcopal Church was last revised in 1979.

Mutual influence

All this is not to say that the Anglican Church has not influenced the Lutheran church. One author explained it this way: "In the face of liturgically deficient American Lutheran agendas, *The Book of Common Prayer* represented a full liturgical resource to which Lutherans could turn especially for prayers and occasional services in English. When Lutherans began working in earnest on a common service in English in the second half of the nineteenth century, they turned to the translations of texts in *The Book of Common Prayer* (including the Lord's Prayer, the Nicene and Apostles' Creeds, and the canticles)."[27] This will explain, for example, why the same collects (short prayers) can be heard in both Lutheran and Episcopal churches. Consider the following two sets of prayers:

1. "Stir up thy power, O Lord, and with great might come among us; and, because we are sorely hindered by our sins, let thy bountiful grace and mercy speedily help and deliver us; through Jesus Christ our Lord, to whom, with thee and the Holy Ghost, be honor and glory, world without end. Amen" (*The Book of Common Prayer,* Collect for Third Sunday of Advent).[28]

2. "Stir up, O Lord, we beseech Thee, Thy power, and come and help us with Thy great might, that by Thy grace whatsoever is hindered by our sins may be speedily accomplished through Thy mercy and satisfaction; who livest and reignest with the Father and the Holy Ghost; ever one God, world without end.

Amen" (*The Lutheran Hymnal,* Collect for the First Sunday in Advent).[29]

3. "Stir up your power, O Lord, and come. Protect us by your strength and save us from the threatening dangers of our sins; for you live and reign with the Father and the Holy Spirit, one God, now and forever. Amen" (*Christian Worship: Manual,* Collect for the First Sunday in Advent).[30]

1. "Almighty and everlasting God, who hatest nothing that thou hast made and dost forgive the sins of all those who are penitent: Create and make in us new and contrite hearts, that we, worthily lamenting our sins and acknowledging our wretchedness, may obtain of thee, the God of all mercy, perfect remission and forgiveness; through Jesus Christ our Lord, who liveth and reigneth with thee and the Holy Spirit, one God, for ever and ever. Amen" (*The Book of Common Prayer,* Collect for Ash Wednesday).[31]

2. "Almighty and everlasting God, who hatest nothing that Thou has made and dost forgive the sins of all those who are penitent, create and make in us new and contrite hearts, that we, worthily lamenting our sins and acknowledging our wretchedness, may obtain of Thee, the God of all mercy, perfect remission and forgiveness; through Jesus Christ Thy Son, our Lord, who liveth and reigneth with Thee and the Holy Spirit, ever one God, world without end. Amen" (*The Lutheran Hymnal,* Collect for Ash Wednesday).[32]

3. "Almighty and merciful God, you never despise what you have made and always forgive those who turn to you. Create in us such new and contrite hearts that we may truly repent of our sins and obtain your full and gracious pardon; through your Son, Jesus Christ our Lord, who lives and reigns with you and the Holy Spirit, one God, now and forever. Amen" (*Christian Worship: Manual,* Collect for Ash Wednesday).[33]

Role of *The Book of Common Prayer*

The Book of Common Prayer is important to Episcopal Church members for a number of reasons. It is the book that contains the liturgical forms for use in a wide range of worship services, from Holy Communion services (called the Eucharist) to burials to ordination services. *The Book of Common Prayer* also serves as a resource book for people's devotional lives. It serves that purpose because it contains the psalms, numerous prayers and collects, and the catechism. Clergy and laity alike point to the long-lasting influence and unifying effect of *The Book of Common Prayer.*

The Book of Common Prayer "is probably the most important and enduring monument of the English Reformation. It has been for centuries a factor second only to episcopacy itself in unifying the Church of England and the Anglican Communion."[34]

United by worship or belief?

But how much does *The Book of Common Prayer* unite members of the Episcopal Church? And how much does it unite the member churches of the Anglican Communion? I posed that first question to Episcopal Church clergy throughout the country by means of a random survey. I invited the clergy to respond to this statement: "As a leader in the Episcopal Church, I believe that the forms of worship, rather than what we believe, unite Episcopalians." Respondents could choose their answer from the following list: A. I very much disagree with that statement; B. I disagree with that statement; C. I somewhat agree with that statement; D. I agree with that statement; E. I very much agree with that statement; or F. Other. As one might expect, the responses were varied. Here is a sampling of those who agreed with that statement:

"I very much agree with that statement. Not limited to 'forms' but more fully 'content' of worship."

"I basically agree with that statement—although in recent years 'issues' of belief or theology or biblical authority have caused tremendous discussion."

"I believe our liturgies unite us in our worship of Almighty God, placing our focus on God, despite the differences we may share about other things."

"I believe this statement is what we have in common but I believe we now see how fragile that seeming unity has been."

Other respondents disagreed with the statement that forms of worship, rather than doctrine, unite Episcopalians:

"The spectrum of what we believe has clearly divided the Episcopal Church. Because of that division our worship can no longer have the uniting effect that it once had. Worship forms are beginning to vary by the theological orientation of the diocese and/or the congregation. Unfortunately many can worship with *The Book of Common Prayer* and not live by the primarily scriptural content of it."

"I believe that the Baptismal Covenant unites Episcopalians."

"It is not the form of worship that matters but the fact of worshiping together as one body that matters."

"We are united principally, by who we worship, and secondarily, by the shared form of that worship. Our model is a family related to a person, not a club whose members subscribe to a creed. But the theological confession presupposed by Christian faith cannot be separated from the form of worship; it's a pervasive and essential component of our liturgy. We encourage everyone to believe the essential doctrines of Christian theology, and strive to exemplify their reasonableness and winsomeness, but we welcome everyone, irrespective of where they might be on their faith journey."

It becomes clear that people on both sides of the issue see the need for worship to reflect theology. That leads to the next question: What is the Anglican approach to theology? The answer to that question is clear. It is a matter of "both/and," not "either/or."

Three-legged stool

"'God Said It. That Settles It.' is not an Episcopalian bumper sticker."[35] That statement comes from a newsletter of the Episcopal Diocese of Southern Virginia. The author went on to explain: "Despite the centrality of the Bible to Episcopal worship, unlike many Protestants, we don't appeal to 'Scripture alone' as *the* authority for faith and life. Scripture, we say, has Primacy; it is the first place to go as an authority for what we believe. Yet, clearly at times the appeal to Scripture alone is insufficient as guide; then reason and tradition are joyfully celebrated."[36]

When did this approach begin? One Episcopalian author wrote: "At the time of the Protestant Reformation, we did not become a confessional church. We did not adopt a series of dogmas that you have to believe in order to be a good Episcopalian. That doesn't mean that we're a church without teachings. We have teachings. We have the Bible. We have our *Book of Common Prayer*. We have our hymnal. We have the Godly Admonitions of our Bishops and we have the decisions of our church councils."[37]

The preceding paragraphs allude to the three-legged stool upon which the Anglican faith rests. The "three-legged stool" is an old expression that describes how Scripture, tradition, and human reason serve as legs that support a seating surface, in this case, the Anglican faith. Tradition (what other Christians have said and written in the past) and reason (what human experience teaches) are also sources of authority in Anglican thinking. The Lutheran reader will immediately notice that *sola Scriptura,* "by Scripture alone," is not a part of Anglican theology. For Anglicans, Scripture is not the sole source of authority.

On its Web site, one Episcopal Church in Washington State gives this answer to the question: How do Episcopalians decide what to believe? "Episcopalians place great faith in religious decisions which are made gradually by balancing all points of view. In matters of faith, Episcopalians achieve this gradual balance by relying on a 'three-legged stool' of scripture, tradition, and reason. No single leg is self-sufficient, and, if any of the others were to be removed, the entire structure would topple. The Bible, or scripture, is the record of God's personal revelation to humanity. Episcopalians take the Bible very seriously, although not always literally, and 80% of their liturgy is scripture arranged for worship. Tradition represents God's ongoing revelation to humanity, which is continually refreshed through the Church's living body of thought. The stream of tradition, carrying staples, such as the creeds and the catechism, gathers force as successive generations of believers bequeath and build upon their hard-won insights. Reason is the God-given power of the human mind to discern truth in scripture, tradition, and daily experience. The interplay of all three—scripture, tradition and reason—gradually shows Episcopalians what to believe about God."[38]

Confessional Lutheranism, on the other hand, sees Scripture as the only source of faith. The Formula of Concord, drafted in 1577, begins with these words: "We believe, teach, and confess that the sole rule and standard according to which all dogmas together with [all] teachers should be estimated and judged are the prophetic and apostolic Scriptures of the Old and of the New Testament alone."[39] The Lutheran Confessions simply express what we find in Scripture. Jesus said about the Scriptures: "Your word is truth" (John 17:17). The apostle Paul explained that the Christian church is "built on the foundation of the apostles and prophets [the human authors of the Bible] with Christ Jesus himself as the chief cornerstone" (Ephesians 2:20). The psalm writer noted that God's Word "is a lamp to my feet and a light for my path" (Psalm 119:105).

The teaching of the Bible

So how does the Episcopal Church view Holy Scripture? The catechism in *The Book of Common Prayer* offers official church teaching by way of these questions and answers:

Q. What is the Old Testament? A. The Old Testament consists of books written by the people of the Old

Covenant, under the inspiration of the Holy Spirit, to show God at work in nature and history.

Q. What is the New Testament? A. The New Testament consists of books written by the people of the New Covenant, under the inspiration of the Holy Spirit, to set forth the life and teachings of Jesus and to proclaim the Good News of the Kingdom for all people.

Q. What is the Apocrypha? A. The Apocrypha is a collection of additional books written by people of the Old Covenant, and used in the Christian church.

Q. Why do we call the Holy Scriptures the Word of God? A. We call them the Word of God because God inspired their human authors and because God still speaks to us through the Bible.[40]

The catechism in *The Book of Common Prayer* presents the Old and New Testaments as being the inspired work of the Holy Spirit. Accordingly, those ordained as priests and deacons in the Episcopal Church must profess acceptance of the Old and New Testaments as God's Word. The oath for those being ordained as priests and deacons in the Episcopal Church contains these words: "I solemnly declare that I do believe the Holy Scriptures of the Old and New Testaments to be the Word of God, and to contain all things necessary to salvation; and I do solemnly engage to conform to the doctrine, discipline, and worship of the Episcopal Church."[41]

Views of the Bible

The affirmation in the ordination vow that the Bible contains "all things necessary to salvation" reads well, but it apparently allows one to conclude that the Bible is reliable when it speaks of salvation but not necessarily when it speaks of matters that are not directly related to salvation. This was borne out when I surveyed Episcopal clergy on their beliefs about the Bible. One question in the survey asked the clergy to state their views of the Bible: Regarding the Bible, I believe that (A) all the Bible is inspired by the Holy Spirit and therefore inerrant; (B) portions of the Bible are inspired and inerrant, others are not; (C) the Bible is a human book, containing important material but not inspired by God; or (D) Other. Most responses were in categories A and D. Here is a sampling of responses:

"I believe that the Bible is the revealed Word of God, inspired by the Holy Spirit but recorded by humankind and therefore subject to error."

"The Bible is the Word of God but not the 'words' of God. The Bible contains all things necessary for salvation."

"The Bible is inspired by the Holy Spirit and contains the inerrant truth, not necessarily the literal word. For example I believe in the truth of the Adam and Eve story but do not believe that they literally existed."

"The Bible is the story of the interaction of God with humanity. It is inspired but not inerrant."

"I take the Bible too seriously to take it literally."

"The Bible is uniquely God's word to us; inspired by the Holy Spirit. It reliably communicates everything necessary for our knowledge of God and his plans and purposes for us, irrespective of whatever errors it might contain by virtue of its being a human, as well as a divine, book."

"Regarding the Bible, I believe that God inspired people in their cultures to write the Bible, editors worked on the final result, and translators gave it their final spin as well."

"Jesus Christ is the incarnate Word of God; the Holy Scriptures of the Old and New Testaments are the written word of God; and the apostolic witness (tradition) is the proclaimed word of God. Although the Holy Scriptures were inspired by the Holy Spirit, these books were written by human authors, and therefore are not 'inerrant.'"

"The Bible is the 'inspired' word of God and contains all that is necessary for salvation. I think generally Episcopalians accept the 'Truth' of the Scriptures without having to agree on their complete historical accuracy. For example, some of the stories of the Old Testament come from ancient legend incorporated into the Hebrew Bible as it was being collected during and after the Exile. The stories of Jesus and the Church as represented in the Gospels and the Book of Acts tell an accurate story, but can be open to interpretation in terms of detail."

"Dear Survey Person: I realize I am firmly in the left-wing of the Episcopal Church; however, that given, your initial questions, it seems to me, did not allow for the ambiguity that characterizes Anglican thinking and theology. They were much too 'right-wrong,' 'true-false,' without allowing for the 'shades of gray' in the choices for answers. Just the first one: I do believe that the Bible is inspired by God and I do believe it is not inerrant. I want one from column A and one from Column B. I pray there are lots of Episcopalians like me instead of those who can choose easily between inerrancy and meaninglessness."

That same person concluded with a quote he attributed to Gertrude Stein: "There ain't no answer. There ain't going to be any answer. There never has been an answer. That's the answer."

This brief sampling of quotes, along with many others not included, indicates that rationalistic literary criticism, a method of interpreting the Bible that denies inspiration and inerrancy, has a strong foothold in the Episcopal Church. One also finds the presence of gospel reductionism, where a person sees truth and certainty in those places of the Bible that speak of God's grace in Christ (the gospel) but allows for inaccuracies and errors in those portions of the Bible that relate historical, scientific, and other information.

Yet a good number of Episcopal clergy responded differently: "All the Bible is inspired by the Holy Spirit."

"All the Bible is inspired by the Holy Spirit and is therefore the authoritative word of God written."

"Holy Scripture is the true and lively Word of God, written by men under the inspiration of the Holy Spirit."

"The Bible was written by humans and inspired by God."

"Holy Scripture is the revealed Word of God. It is all inspired by God. We don't get to pick and choose which parts are revelation."

It is striking to read such divergent views on Scripture from those called to teach in the Episcopal Church. And it follows that when a church has different views on the nature of the Bible, different views of what the Bible teaches will also exist in that church. But could that diversity of views possibly include the most important teaching of the Bible, salvation? When Scripture is not the sole foundation of a church and the only guide to one's faith, anything is possible.

Review: During the early years of the Reformation, the Church of England adopted worship forms from the Lutheran church. Later in America, some Lutheran worship forms reflected Anglican influence. These events explain the similarity one can find in Lutheran and Episcopalian liturgies.

The Book of Common Prayer is a unifying force in the Episcopal Church and the Anglican Communion. Like the Roman Catholic Church, the Episcopal Church looks beyond Scripture for sources of authority in matters of faith and life. In addition to Scripture, human reason and tradition guide the church and its members.

While the church professes belief in the inspiration of the Bible, the language of the church's catechism makes it possible for clergy and laity to limit inspiration to matters of salvation only. In this regard, the Episcopal Church mirrors the thinking of many Christian denominations but not confessional Lutheranism.

ANGLICAN APPROACH TO THEOLOGY: SALVATION
and the Sacraments

Preview: The Episcopal Church is considered a Christian church because it proclaims the gospel of Jesus Christ and administers the sacraments. While the church points people to Jesus Christ as the world's Savior, clergy comments reveal the inroads of universalism, the belief that there is salvation apart from faith in Jesus Christ. The Episcopal Church acknowledges two sacraments: Holy Baptism and Holy Communion. Episcopalians also identify five sacramental rites.

In the survey I conducted, I asked the respondents to complete this statement: Regarding my own salvation, I believe that . . . , and add comments. Here is the comment of one Episcopal priest: "Our salvation is through Christ Jesus. By his rising to life again, he has won for us everlasting life. Must a Christian do good works to be saved? No. Does a Christian do good works? Absolutely." Contrast that statement with this one by another priest: "Salvation is solely the business of God—I don't know." Can the teachings of the Episcopal Church be broad enough to allow both views?

Once again, one needs to turn to the official teachings of the church as they are contained in the catechism in *The Book of Common Prayer.* The section entitled "Sin and Redemption" contains these questions and answers:

Q. What is redemption? A. Redemption is the act of God which sets us free from the power of evil, sin and death.

Q. Who do we believe is the Messiah? A. The Messiah, or Christ, is Jesus of Nazareth, the only Son of God.

Q. What is the great importance of Jesus' suffering and death? A. By his obedience, even to suffering and death, Jesus made the offering which we could not make; in him we are freed from the power of sin and reconciled to God.

Q. What is the significance of Jesus' resurrection? A. By his resurrection, Jesus overcame death and opened for us the way of eternal life.

Q. How can we share in his victory over sin, suffering, and death? A. We share in his victory when we are baptized into the New Covenant and become living members of Christ.[42]

Official teachings of the Episcopal Church clearly point to Jesus Christ as the way of salvation. Yet one will find Episcopal Church priests expressing varied views on the topic of salvation. Respondents to my survey were asked to complete the statement: Regarding my own salvation, I believe that _____. Respondents could choose (A) Jesus Christ won my salvation completely through his holy life, innocent death, and resurrection; (B) Jesus Christ lived and died to take away my sins, but living a Christian life and doing good works contributes to my salvation; or (C) other. The majority of respondents chose Option A, although a fair number did choose B and C. Here is a sampling of all comments:

"Our response to this overwhelming love is to do good works. They are the fruit of my reaction to Jesus' love. To have either A or B is too simplistic."

"Jesus Christ won my salvation on the Cross, but not through theologies of atonement."

"Jesus Christ won my salvation completely through his holy life, innocent death, and resurrection. I can contribute to or detract from my experience of eternal salvation through my behavior."

"Regarding my own salvation, I accept Jesus Christ as my Savior; I put my whole trust in his grace and love; and I follow and obey him as my Lord."

"I'm not sure that individual salvation is the point of Jesus' teaching, nor his work."

"I regard my salvation only by extension to that of all human beings—Jesus Christ's life, death and resurrection was for the salvation of all humankind. My knowledge, acceptance, and 'living and doing good works' have nothing to do with it."

"Jesus Christ lived and died to take away my sins, but living a Christian life and doing good works contributes to the health of my soul."

Salvation for others

After asking Episcopal Church clergy how they viewed their own salvation, I asked them to respond to this statement: Regarding salvation in general, I believe that (A) salvation and eternal life are limited to those who acknowledge Jesus Christ as their Savior; (B) salvation and eternal life will be enjoyed by those who worship God, however they may define god in their culture; or (C) other. The respondents were nearly evenly split between A and B/C.

Those who chose the Option A provided very few comments, but here is a sampling:

"However, I am also of the mind that because God intends to reconcile all of creation to himself, and His grace exceeds my limited imagination, that He has a way to bring nonbelievers into the fold. For example, we imagine that Christ 'descended to the dead' after his death to offer salvation to those who had not yet been saved." This view of Jesus' descent into hell is one that parallels Roman Catholic teaching and disagrees with confessional Lutheranism.

"Provided that we understand that it is God's prerogative. Old Testament Jews could not 'acknowledge Jesus' per se, but they could have faith in Him as the promised Messiah and instrument of salvation."

"Answer is **A.** However, as Paul prophesies in Romans 14:11—for it is written, 'As I live, says the Lord, every knee shall bow to me, and every tongue shall give praise to God.' This of course is at the resurrection."

Most of the comments on the survey came from those who chose the "other" category. Here is a sampling of their thoughts:

"Salvation is a fact accomplished by Jesus Christ. One merely has to accept it (receive the gift)—either in this world or the next."

"I can't see God rejecting someone because they did not know of Jesus, or an incompetent was sent to evangelize them, etc. Who gets salvation is God's problem, not mine."

"I know that those who claim and accept Jesus Christ as their Lord and Savior are assured of salvation. . . . I leave the rest up to God and suspect his kingdom is big enough for all devout believers."

"God sent his only Son into the world that all the world might be saved. I believe that the world will be saved through Jesus Christ. Saying that salvation 'will be limited to those who acknowledge Jesus Christ as their Savior' is poorly stated. Who is doing the limiting? It sounds as if it is God who is being limited."

"Salvation is solely the business of God—I don't know."

"Perhaps we 'Christians' have not always been the ambassadors that we were sent to be. If we have turned people from Christ by our actions (invading foreign lands, conquering people, forcing conversions under pain of death, burning one another at the stake, child sexual abuse, verbal abuse), then would God send non-Christians to hell because of our failure? I believe that God is Love and he who abides in love abides in God and God in him/her."

"Salvation is through Jesus Christ. How this will work for godly people who do not know Christ or are faithful members of other religions is not really my business, but I'm sure God has it figured out."

"The revelation Christians have received in Scripture and in Christ would imply that there is salvation only through Christ, but it's possible God has another plan."

"Salvation is enjoyed by those who are in relationship with God (not necessarily through Jesus Christ) and that God desires to give eternal life to all."

It is apparent from clergy comments that there are different views in the Episcopal Church regarding the matter of who enjoys forgiveness of sins and eternal life. As we have shown, the catechism of the Episcopal Church underscores the redeeming work of Christ. The confession and proclamation of Christ crucified places the Episcopal Church under the umbrella of the Christian church. However, there are a fair number of clergy who go beyond their church's teachings and embrace a form of universalism, the idea that all people will ultimately enjoy salvation.

What could lead to such a conclusion? In a word, *incarnation.*

The indwelling of Christ

Incarnation refers to the miracle of the Son of God becoming man. Isaiah's famous prophecy foretold this: "The virgin will be with child and will give birth to a son, and will call him Immanuel" (Isaiah 7:14). In his account of Jesus' birth, the apostle Matthew explains that *Immanuel* means "God with us" (Matthew 1:23). The apostle Paul stated by inspiration of the Holy Spirit that "in Christ all the fullness of the Deity lives in bodily form" (Colossians 2:9). The miracle at Bethlehem is that the almighty and eternal Son of God took on human flesh. That is incarnation.

Another miracle takes place when the Holy Spirit brings a person to faith in Jesus Christ. Scripture says that God dwells within that person. Jesus said, "If anyone loves me, he will obey my teaching. My Father will love him, and we will come to him and make our home with him" (John 14:23). The apostle Paul declared: "I have been crucified with Christ and I no longer live, but Christ lives in me" (Galatians 2:20). That same apostle asked: "Don't you know that you yourselves are God's temple and that God's Spirit lives in you?" (1 Corinthians 3:16).

Based on what Scripture says, confessional Lutherans believe that God dwells in the hearts of his followers. On the other hand, some Episcopalians believe that Christ dwells in every person, Christian and non-Christian alike. By and large, people with that viewpoint look to Jesus' parable of the sheep and the goats for the basis of their belief. In the parable, the believers who were commended for their acts of love asked Jesus: "Lord, when did we see you hungry and feed you, or thirsty and give you something to drink? When we did we see you a stranger and invite you in, or needing clothes and clothe you? When did we see you sick or in prison and go to visit you?" (Matthew 25:37-39). They received the answer: "I tell you the truth, whatever you did for one of the least of these brothers of mine, you did for me" (verse 40).

In that same parable, the unbelievers who were condemned to hell asked a similar question: "Lord, when did we see you hungry or thirsty or a stranger or needing clothes or sick or in prison, and did not help you?" (verse 44) They received this answer from Jesus: "I tell you the truth, whatever you did not do for one of the least of these, you did not do for me" (verse 45).

Some Episcopalians conclude from Jesus' statements that he dwells in all people, that "the least of these" refers not just to believers but to believers and unbelievers alike. Rev. James L. Jelinek presently serves as the bishop of the Minnesota Diocese of the Episcopal Church. In an interview with the author, Jelinek said: "Incarnation happens in everyone. God indwells everyone. Our task is to keep seeking someone until we see the Christ in them. We can't stop because the person is mean and nasty. When we see the Christ, we serve the Christ."[43] Jelinek stated that his words reflect one of the questions asked of a person being baptized according to the baptismal form in *The*

Book of Common Prayer: "Will you seek and serve Christ in all persons, loving your neighbor as yourself?"[44]

Rev. Paul G. Rider is the priest-in-charge at St. John Episcopal Church in Mankato, Minnesota. When asked about the Episcopalian understanding of the indwelling of Christ in all people, he responded: "We treat each person as if each person were Christ. We treat that person with dignity, love, and forgiveness."[45] He acknowledged that I might wonder why the Episcopal Church still baptizes and evangelizes if, in fact, Christ dwells in all people. He assured me that we would have to meet for quite a while longer to resolve that issue.

Jesus is the Savior

Confessional Lutheranism understands and professes that there is salvation in Jesus Christ alone. The Augsburg Confession states: "Also they [our churches] teach that men cannot be justified before God by their own strength, merits, or works, but are freely justified for Christ's sake, through faith, when they believe that they are received into favor, and that their sins are forgiven for Christ's sake, who, by His death, has made satisfaction for our sins. This faith God imputes for righteousness in His sight. Rom. 3 and 4."[46] Jesus said clearly: "I am the way and the truth and the life. No one comes to the Father except through me" (John 14:6). Holy Scripture says about Jesus: "Salvation is found in no one else, for there is no other name under heaven given to men by which we must be saved" (Acts 4:12). But when the biblical teaching of the indwelling of Christ in Christians is broadened to include all people, it is easy to hold out the hope that non-Christians will be saved. This idea is not uncommon among Episcopalians.

But how do people come to faith and grow in faith? In spite of what we have just heard, Episcopalians do point to the sacraments for the answer.

How many sacraments?

While Roman Catholics recognize seven sacraments, Lutherans see only two. Officially, Episcopalians side with Lutherans regarding the number of sacraments. For Lutherans and Episcopalians, there are the Sacrament of Holy Baptism and the Sacrament of Holy Communion. To complicate matters, though, Episcopalians speak of five additional sacramental rites. And to further complicate matters, some Episcopalians refer to the five sacramental rites as five additional sacraments. An Episcopal Church in Texas included this information on its FAQ (Frequently Asked Questions) page on its Web site: "What are the Sacraments of the Episcopal Church? Baptism, Confirmation, the Eucharist, Holy Matrimony, Reconciliation ("confession"), Ordination and Unction of the Sick. Of these, Baptism and Holy Eucharist are considered 'necessary' sacraments . . . the others are 'conditional' sacraments (i.e., they are not required of all persons, but apply in certain situations)."[47]

Holy Baptism

The catechism in *The Book of Common Prayer* officially defines the faith of the Episcopal Church regarding Baptism. It says:

Q. What is Holy Baptism? A. Holy Baptism is the sacrament by which God adopts us as his children and makes us members of Christ's Body, the Church, and inheritors of the kingdom of God.

Q. What is the outward and visible sign in Baptism? A. The outward and visible sign in Baptism is water, in which the person is baptized in the Name of the Father, and of the Son, and of the Holy Spirit.

Q. What is the inward and spiritual grace in Baptism? A. The inward and spiritual grace in Baptism is union with Christ in his death and resurrection, birth into God's family, the Church, forgiveness of sins, and new life in the Holy Spirit.[48]

The catechism in *The Book of Common Prayer* explains Baptism as a means of grace whereby the Holy Spirit works saving faith in people and brings Christ's forgiveness into their lives. The church baptizes both adults and infants, recognizing people's natural sinfulness and need for forgiveness. There is no controversy in the church regarding the manner in which water is applied in Baptism. Sprinkling and immersion are both considered appropriate, although sprinkling is much more common.

While the catechism of *The Book of Common Prayer* may be clear on the nature and benefits of Baptism, Anglican individuality also expresses itself also in the area of Baptism. Witness these statements from Episcopal parishes regarding Baptism:

From an Episcopal church in Atlanta: "Baptism does not make you 'a child of God'—you were born a child of God. Baptism makes you a member of the Church, the community of faith that treasures God's self-introduction in Jesus Christ. Consequently, baptism doesn't 'save' you; rather it introduces you into a community in which you're likely to have the sort of encounter with God in Christ that awakens you to your salvation."[49]

From an Episcopal church in Virginia: "Baptism is a sign of belief in Jesus. It symbolizes burial and resurrection, and thus is the mark of a believer's identification with Christ. Logically, baptism ought to follow belief, which is the case with adult Baptism. But coming out of the Jewish tradition of circumcision, Christian parents include their children in the external expressions of faith. The Scripture promises that if we 'train up a child in the way he should go, when he is old enough he will not depart from it' (Proverbs 22:6). And thus for centuries parents have had their children baptized in the confidence that God will bring the same children into a mature, vibrant Christian faith."[50]

And finally from an Episcopal church in Texas: "There is only one reason for baptizing a child in the name of Jesus Christ—the parents have made Jesus Christ the head of their household. Such families have a special relationship (called the New Covenant) with God in which they want their children to share. The Lord Jesus has given Baptism as the outward sign of this relationship."[51]

Regardless of local views about the nature of Baptism, it appears that all Episcopal parishes recognize the validity of baptisms that are performed in other Christian churches. Therefore, an Episcopal church will not rebaptize a person who was baptized in the Roman Catholic Church and now wishes to join the Episcopal Church. The only requirement is that the details of the baptism that was performed in a Roman Catholic parish are to be entered into the records of the Episcopal parish.

Holy Eucharist

The second sacrament of the Episcopal Church is the Holy Eucharist. Lutherans know this sacrament better as Holy Communion or the Lord's Supper, but Eucharist is the name the Episcopal Church uses almost exclusively. The name comes from the Greek word *eucharisteo,* which means "to give thanks." The biblical accounts of the institution of Holy Communion explain that Jesus gave thanks before giving the bread and the cup to his disciples. Therefore, Episcopalians (and a few other churches) refer to Holy Communion as "the giving of thanks" or Holy Eucharist.

The catechism in *The Book of Common Prayer* offers this information on Episcopalian belief regarding the Holy Eucharist.

Q. What is the Holy Eucharist? A. The Holy Eucharist is the sacrament commanded by Christ for the continual remembrance of his life, death, and resurrection, until his coming again.

Q. Why is the Eucharist called a sacrifice? A. Because the Eucharist, the Church's sacrifice of praise and thanksgiving, is the way by which the sacrifice of Christ is made present, and in which he unites us to his one offering of himself.

Q. By what other names is this service known? A. The Holy Eucharist is called the Lord's Supper, and Holy Communion; it is also known as the Divine Liturgy, the Mass, and the Great Offering.

Q. What is the inward and spiritual grace given in the Eucharist? A. The inward and spiritual grace in the Holy Communion is the Body and Blood of Christ given to his people, and received by faith.

Q. What are the benefits which we receive in the Lord's Supper? A. The benefits we receive are the forgiveness of our sins, the strengthening of our union with Christ and one another, and the foretaste of the heavenly banquet which is our nourishment in eternal life.[52]

Through its catechism, the Episcopal Church officially states that the Eucharist is a sacrament that contains outward and visible signs and inward and spiritual graces. While confessional Lutherans believe in the "real presence" of Jesus' body and blood in the Sacrament, the Episcopal Church speaks of the "real" presence of Jesus' body and blood in the Sacrament. Trying to understand what the Episcopal Church means by the "real" presence of Jesus' body and blood is not an easy task.

The nature of the Eucharist

Determining what the Episcopal Church teaches regarding the nature of the Eucharist can be difficult because over the years the church has put forth various views. That is not surprising considering the origin of the Anglican Church. As one Episcopalian priest reminded me, "Thomas Cranmer combined a couple of faith traditions with his liturgies."[53] Those different faith traditions became evident in the different versions of *The Book of Common Prayer*. In the first *Book of Common Prayer* (1549), the Anglican Church rejected the Roman Catholic Church's teaching of transubstantiation, the belief that the earthly elements of bread and wine change into Christ's body and blood. Part of the liturgy for the Holy Eucharist (in the old English) stated: "He hath left in those holy Misteries, as a pledge of his love, and a continuall remembraunce of the same his owne blessed body, and precious bloud, for us to fede upon spiritually."[54] That liturgy from the first *Book of*

Common Prayer taught worshipers that the Eucharist involved the spiritual eating of Jesus' body and blood. Three years later, the second *Book of Common Prayer* "encouraged the idea that the presence of Christ was not in the sacrament, but only in the heart of the believer."[55] That idea came out in these words of the liturgy: ". . . for as the benifite is great, if with a truly penitent heart and lively faith, we receive that holy Sacrament (for then we spirutallye eate the flesh of Christ, and drynke hys bloud, then we dwell in Christ, we be one with Christ, and Christ with us). . . ."[56]

In the 1789 *Book of Common Prayer,* the first prayer book for the Episcopal Church, the liturgy for the Eucharist included petitions that the communicants "may worthily receive the most precious Body and Blood of thy Son Jesus Christ."[57]

In 1801 the Episcopal Church's General Convention took place in Trenton, New Jersey. The convention adopted the Articles of Religion, a confessional document for a nonconfessional church. In Article XXVIII, "Of the Lord's Supper," one finds these statements:

The Supper of the Lord is not only a sign of the love that Christians ought to have among themselves one to another; but rather it is a Sacrament of our Redemption by Christ's death: in so much that to such as rightly, worthily, and with faith, receive the same, the Bread which we break is a partaking of the Body of Christ; and likewise the Cup of blessing is a partaking of the Blood of Christ.

Transubstantiation (or the change of the substance of Bread and Wine) in the Supper of the Lord, cannot be proved by Holy Writ; but is repugnant to the plain words of Scripture, overthroweth the nature of a Sacrament, and hath given occasion to many superstitions.

The Body of Christ is given, taken, and eaten, in the Supper, only after an heavenly and spiritual manner. And the means whereby the Body of Christ is received and eaten in the Supper, is Faith.

The Sacrament of the Lord's Supper was not by Christ's ordinance reserved, carried about, lifted up, or worshiped.[58]

Those statements from the Articles of Religion clearly reject transubstantiation and speak of communicants receiving the Lord's body and blood "only after an heavenly and spiritual manner." That view sees the Sacrament similar to what the Reformed church teaches, where Jesus' body and blood are thought to be present only in a spiritual manner.

As noted previously, *The Book of Common Prayer* (1979) presently used by the Episcopal Church teaches this regarding the Eucharist:

Q. What is the outward and visible sign in the Eucharist?
A. The outward and visible sign in the Eucharist is bread and wine, given and received according to Christ's command.

Q. What is the inward and spiritual grace given in the Eucharist? A. The inward and spiritual grace in the Holy Communion is the Body and Blood of Christ given to his people, and received by faith.[59]

Contemporary understanding

So what do present-day Episcopalians believe they receive in the Eucharist? It depends on whom you ask. One Episcopal priest told me: "Most Episcopalians would believe in a form of transubstantiation. Definitely the real presence. Understanding the Eucharist is not a requirement of faith. I let God work out the details."[60]

In an article of *Catholic Answers,* Edwina Conason interviewed an Episcopal priest to seek out his views on the Eucharist. Here is part of her interview:

Q. What is the definition of a sacrament in the Episcopal Church? A. The simple definition that you teach children in confirmation classes [is]: "A sacrament is an outward and visible sign of an inward and spiritual grace." So what we say is, there are two parts to the sacrament that you can actually see going on, like the joining of hands, the exchange of rings, . . . the bread and wine that become the Body and Blood of Christ that are distributed at the holy Eucharist. And then the inward part of what really is happening. And, of course, at Eucharist, the theology of the Episcopal Church is that the bread and wine actually become the Real Presence of Christ, and that when you receive that Sacrament you receive his Body and Blood, not bread and wine.

Q. In reality? Or spiritually? A. In every way except physically.

Q. I know Episcopalians who believe in consubstantiation. A. The theology in the Episcopal Church talks of "Real Presence." Jesus said, "This is my body." He didn't say, "This is a memorial of me." He didn't say anything other than simply, "You take the bread, you bless it, you break it, you give it to the people. You take the wine, you bless it, you give it to the people. And it is my body and it is my blood." He doesn't say in which way it is. . . .

If you take the Catholic sacrament—or an Episcopal sacrament or Baptist or anybody else's—and run it through a chemical lab, it's still going to be bread and wine. In the Roman Catholic theology they have what they call the "accident" of the sacrament, and they don't mean, "Oops, you caught us." They mean accident like it's an underlying thing, that it really is the Body and Blood of Christ, even physically, except it's all underlying. It's got this bread and wine that still sort of shows up somehow.

And in order to avoid that sort of complicating how-are-you-going-to-explain-it mess, we say it's Christ's Body and Blood in every way except physically. Because we know when you run that chemical test and prove it's not flesh and blood, it's still bread and wine.[61]

Those are the thoughts of one priest, but does he speak for all Episcopalians? Read on. An Episcopal church in Tennessee makes this statement on its Web site: "The Episcopal Church does not believe that the bread and wine physically change into the Body and Blood of Christ, though it must be noted that there are some Episcopalians who hold this belief."[62]

An Episcopal church in New York State explains the sacrament this way: "The Episcopal Church (together with the Orthodox and Roman Catholic communions) teaches that the Sacrament is objective, not dependent upon the subjective belief or understanding of any participant in the liturgy; it is the 'real presence' of Christ within and for us. However, in the Anglican tradition initiated in the Elizabethan Settlement, belief in the doctrine of the real presence is not prerequisite to receiving Communion."[63]

An Episcopal priest who teaches at a university shared these thoughts with me in our correspondence:

"It's because I believe that God works extra-sacramentally as well (God's grace is not limited by God's sacraments) that I have no problem receiving the Lord's Supper in a Baptist Church, for example. The service is at least the memorial they claim it to be; whether or not it is 'equal' to receiving holy communion at a Eucharist is a matter for God's judgment, not mine. I'm all for 'open communion' but not for a confounding of religious traditions or for acting as if all traditions are somehow 'the same' (they may be—but I have no way of knowing that). I can meditate with Buddhists and would welcome them to pray with me, but I would not want a Buddhist attempting to preside at Holy Eucharist—nor would I attempt to preside at a sesshin [a Buddhist retreat that focuses on meditation].

"Perhaps I should feel differently (I used 'feel' advisedly), but I don't. We are in an 'anything goes' culture: I think the role of traditions, of standards, of orders of worship need not to be lost. At the same time, I don't think our differences are most important: all human beings are created by God and called to life in God. God speaks in a myriad of ways, through different traditions."

The previous statements from churches and clergy demonstrate that there is diversity of thought in the Episcopal Church regarding the nature of the Eucharist. By contrast, confessional Lutheranism declares: "*Of the Supper of the Lord* they [our churches] teach that the Body and Blood of Christ are truly present, and are distributed to those who eat in the Supper of the Lord; and they reject those that teach otherwise."[64] Finally, Jesus said: "This is my body. . . . This is my blood" (Matthew 26:26,28).

Eucharistic practices

While the Episcopal Church has divergent views on the nature of the Eucharist, the church is united in that it practices "open Communion." That means that the reception of the Sacrament is not restricted to members of the church. The only restriction one finds is that those who wish to receive the Sacrament be baptized into the Christian faith. The following statements from Episcopal Church worship service bulletins and Web sites illustrate various practices regarding the Sacrament.

"All persons are welcome at the Altar and at the communion stations to receive the Sacrament of the Body and Blood of our Lord. . . . If you want to receive the wine by intinction (dipping the wafer), please hold the wafer and wait for the second chalice. You may also receive Communion in only one form. To receive a blessing only, cross your arms over your chest as you kneel or stand."[65]

"We are an inclusive church family, in the Anglican tradition, that celebrates God's diversity. Whoever you are, whatever your origin, wherever you are on your spiritual pilgrimage, you are one of us; you are a child of God, made in God's image. There are no 'entrance exams' in this church. As far as we are concerned, everyone has a reservation at the Savior's Table. You are not only welcomed, but encouraged to come forward at the time of Communion to receive the Blessed Sacrament."[66]

"Holy Communion is open to all who wish to receive. This is Christ's Altar, not the Episcopal Church's and all are welcome at Christ's feast.[67]

"All baptized are welcome to make their communion at the altar; we are all guests of God, whose table this is."[68]

Response of confessional Lutheranism

While the Episcopal Church practices "open Communion," confessional Lutheranism espouses "close(d) Communion." *This We Believe,* a confessional document of the Wisconsin Evangelical Lutheran Synod, states:

We believe that those whose confession of faith reveals that they are united in the doctrines of Scripture will express their fellowship in Christ as occasion permits (Ephesians 4:3). They may express their fellowship by joint worship, by joint proclamation of the gospel, by joining in Holy Communion, by joint prayer, and by joint church work. God directs believers not to practice religious fellowship with those whose confession and actions reveal that they teach, tolerate, support, or defend error (2 John 10,11). When error appears in the church, Christians will try to preserve their fellowship by patiently admonishing the offenders, in the hope that they will turn from their error (2 Timothy 1:25,26; Titus 3:10). But the Lord commands believers not to practice church fellowship with people who persist in teaching or adhering to beliefs that are false (Romans 16:17,18).[69]

The Lutheran Church—Missouri Synod officially makes similar statements:

In keeping with the principle that the celebration and reception of the Lord's Supper is a confession of the unity of faith, while at the same time recognizing that there will be instances when sensitive pastoral care needs to be exercised, the Synod has established an official practice requiring 'that pastors and congregations of The Lutheran Church—Missouri Synod, except in situations of emergency and in special cases of pastoral care, commune individuals of only those synods which are now in fellowship with us.' By following this practice whereby only those individuals who are members of the Synod or of a church body with which the Synod is in altar and pulpit fellowship are ordinarily communed, pastors and congregations preserve the integrity of their witness to the Gospel of Christ as it is revealed in the Scriptures and confessed in the Lutheran confessional writings.[70]

Applying those statements on church fellowship to our relation with the Episcopal Church leads to these conclusions: Because confessional Lutheran churches and the Episcopal Church are not "united in the doctrines of Scripture" or in "fellowship" with one another, they are not able to do the things they could if they were united in Scripture, namely, worship together, pray together, commune together, and carry out church work together. The fact that confessional Lutherans do not enjoy fellowship with a visible church like the Episcopal Church does not mean that confessional Lutherans consider Episcopalians to be outside the holy Christian church.

It is important to understand the difference between the invisible church (the holy Christian church) and visible churches like the Episcopal Church and Lutheran churches. The invisible church consists of all those people throughout the world who trust in Jesus Christ as their Savior. Because God alone can look into the heart and see faith, that gathering of believers is referred to as the invisible church. By contrast, visible churches are those gatherings where you can see who the members are. Visible churches have statements and creeds and confessions that explain what they stand for. And people who join visible churches imply by their membership that they believe what their church teaches.

And so when a confessional Lutheran pastor is not able to commune an Episcopalian visitor to his church, it is not done with the attitude that the visitor is not a Christian. No, the primary reason is the lack of a common confession and, therefore, a lack of fellowship between the visitor's church body and the pastor's church body. The Episcopalian visitor represents his or her church body. Communing with confessional Lutherans would say, "I am one with all of you in our beliefs." This would not be true. The Episcopalian visitor might share a common faith in Jesus as Savior, but God alone knows that. It is not our responsibility to determine who is and who is not a member of the invisible church. We mortals are confined to examine the teachings of visible churches. When we examine the teachings of a confessional Lutheran church and the Episcopal Church, we find lack of agreement on what the Bible teaches. If members of those visible churches were to commune together, they would be expressing a unity that does not exist.

Similarly, a confessional Lutheran will not commune in an Episcopal Church because that action would be saying, "I am one with all of you." Again, while that might be a true statement regarding our common membership in the invisible church, we are limited to working with one another as members of visible churches and on the basis of our churches' confessions.

Scripture explains what we are to do in regard to visible churches. It says to "test the spirits to see whether they are from God" (1 John 4:1), and "watch out for those who cause divisions and put obstacles in your way that are contrary to the teaching you have learned. Keep away from them" (Romans 16:17). Unfortunately, some of those from whom we "keep away" misunderstand our actions and wrongly conclude that we consider them outside the invisible church. That misunderstanding is unfortunate, because we are simply trying to apply scriptural principles to them as members of a visible church that does not share our teachings.

Sacramental rites
In addition to the sacraments of Holy Baptism and Holy Eucharist, the Episcopal Church recognizes five "sacramental rites:" confirmation, ordination, holy matrimony, penance, and

unction. (Unction refers to the application of oil or the laying on of hands to bring healing to the sick.) The Roman Catholic Church calls these sacramental rites sacraments. As noted at the beginning of this chapter, there are some within the Episcopal Church who also call the sacramental rites sacraments. They describe them as conditional sacraments, or sacraments that are not necessary for every person. In explaining how these sacramental rites differ from the sacraments, *The Book of Common Prayer* states: "Although they are means of grace, they are not necessary for all persons in the same way that Baptism and the Eucharist are."[71]

While there may be differences of opinion in the Episcopal Church regarding the nature of the Eucharist, the differences are even more pronounced when it comes to matters of sexuality. We will focus on this, among other things, in the next chapter.

Review: The Episcopal Church is considered a Christian church because it proclaims the gospel of Jesus Christ and administers the sacraments. Jesus' holy life and sacrificial death are held up as the payment for the world's sins. Faith in Jesus Christ is seen as the means by which people benefit from Jesus' redeeming work.

However, some clergy maintain that it is not essential for people to believe in Jesus Christ as their Savior in order to enjoy salvation. That is a major difference from confessional Lutheranism and historic Christian belief.

Like the Lutheran church, the Episcopal Church officially recognizes two sacraments: Holy Baptism and Holy Communion. While confessional Lutherans believe in the real presence of the Lord's body and blood (the bread and wine are joined with body and blood in the reception of Holy Communion), the Episcopal Church holds to a variety of understandings.

The official teaching of the Episcopal church speaks of the Lord being present in the sacrament, but the general wording of their statement of faith opens the door to understanding the Lord's presence in various ways. The most common understanding parallels that of Reformed churches, namely, that the Lord's body and blood are not physically present in the sacrament. Some seem to understand the sacrament like the Roman Catholics, and others, like confessional Lutherans. Open Communion is the general practice of the Episcopal Church.

In addition to the two sacraments, the Episcopal Church also acknowledges five sacramental rites: confirmation, ordination, holy matrimony, penance, and unction.

5 THE EPISCOPAL CHURCH AND THE ISSUES OF
Homosexuality and Abortion

Preview: The Episcopal Church is divided over the issue of homosexuality. Recent developments in the church have strained relations in the worldwide Anglican Communion.

At the national level, the Episcopal Church is politically active in defending a woman's right to have an abortion. There is division in the church over this issue also.

If there is one issue that has divided the Episcopal Church and generated criticism from other churches, including churches within the Anglican Communion, it is homosexuality. Within the last 30 years, there has been growing acceptance of homosexuality in the Episcopal Church, even to the degree of ordaining an openly gay man to the office of bishop.

The last 30 years

The history of the Episcopal Church's approval of homosexuality and the resulting tensions in the Anglican Communion is well-documented. "Experimentation with blessings of same sex relationships had begun as early as 1973 within North America."[72] Formal church statements would not come until years later. The 1978 Lambeth Conference adopted this statement in a resolution on human sexuality: "While we reaffirm heterosexuality as the scriptural norm, we recognize the need for deep and dispassionate study of the question of homosexuality, which would take seriously both the teaching of Scripture and the results of scientific and medical research. The Church, recognizing the need for pastoral concern for those who are homosexual, encourages dialogue with them."[73] The Lambeth Conference in 1988 did little more than reaffirm the 1978 resolution. Yet, during that ten-year interval, momentum was building for the first ordination of an openly gay man to the priesthood. That took place in New Jersey in 1989. That ordination, and subsequent ones, caught the attention of the worldwide Anglican Communion, to say the least. The 1998 Lambeth Conference approved a resolution on human sexuality, which stated that it "recognizes that there are among us persons who experience themselves as having a homosexual orientation. Many of these are members of the Church and are seeking the pastoral care, moral direction of the Church, and God's transforming power for the living of their lives and the ordering of relationships. We commit ourselves to listen to the experience of homosexual persons and we wish to assure them that they are loved by God and that all baptized, believing and faithful persons, regardless of sexual orientation, are full members of the Body of Christ."[74]

The Conference also said that "while rejecting homosexual practice as incompatible with Scripture," we call on "all our people to minister pastorally and sensitively to all, irrespective of sexual orientation and to condemn irrational fear of homosexuals, violence within marriage, and any trivialization and commercialization of sex."[75] Perhaps most important at this time, the Conference resolved that it "cannot advise the legitimizing or blessing of same sex unions nor ordaining those involved in same gender unions."[76]

Recall that the Lambeth Conference is one of the four instruments of unity that invite and encourage cooperation within the Anglican Communion. Would the Episcopal Church listen and follow this advice, or would diversity of thought and practice enter the picture? It would not take long to find the answer.

Recent Episcopal Church developments

In the year 2000, the General Convention of the Episcopal Church formally recognized committed relationships other than marriage. One of the resolutions that was passed was "to acknowledge that while issues of human sexuality are not yet resolved, there are couples living in marriage and in other committed relationships within the Body of Christ."[77] In June 2003 the New Hampshire Diocese of the Episcopal Church elected Rev. V. Gene Robinson as its bishop. Because one of the Episcopal Church's canons (church laws) requires that any election of a bishop that takes place within 120 days of the church's General Convention needs to be ratified at the convention, the issue of Robinson's election came before the General Convention that was meeting in Minneapolis, Minnesota, in July 2003. Both the House of Deputies and the House of Bishops confirmed Robinson's election to the office of bishop. Robinson was invested into his office in March 2004.

Robinson's biography on his diocesan Web site states that he "lives with his partner . . . who is employed by the State of New Hampshire's Department of Safety."[78] Robinson is divorced from his wife.

In addition to Robinson's confirmation as bishop, the 2003 General Convention also resolved to reaffirm a previous resolution that stated, "We expect such relationships [i.e., gay] will be characterized by fidelity, monogamy, mutual affection and respect, careful, honest communication, and the holy love which enables those in such relationships to see in each other the image of God" and that "we recognize that local faith communities are operating within the bounds of our common life as they explore and experience liturgies celebrating and blessing same-sex unions."[79] Clearly, the Episcopal Church was taking action that would strain relations within the Anglican Communion and cause difficulties within its own church body.

Division in the Episcopal Church

One of the items in my survey to Episcopal Church clergy was this: I view homosexuality as (A) an alternative lifestyle not condemned by God; (B) sinful behavior; or (C) other.

Here is a sampling of opinions from those who support homosexuality:

"God made homosexual persons that way in the mystery of God. To be in a loving, committed relationship with another person (or seeking such a relationship) is to be honored and encouraged as it is with heterosexual persons."

"I believe that homosexuality is a biological (not lifestyle) variation, and that God does not condemn it. I believe God wants the same thing from homosexuals that God wants from all of us: faithfulness, charity, and doing our best to live the Christian life as described by Jesus Christ and Paul."

"Saint Paul suggests in his Epistle to the Galatians that in Christ 'there is neither Jew nor Greek, there is neither slave nor free, there is neither male nor female,' and by extension of his logic (and God's Word) there is neither straight nor gay. On the other hand, homosexuality, as it is practiced by those who are not in Christ but prefer the counsel of profane society, is sin."

"It is the way God made some people and everything that God has made is good. It not an 'alternative,' as there is no choice, and it is not a 'lifestyle;' it is a life."

"Part of the wonderful diversity reflecting the image of God."

"A variation within the range of God's creation. Like all sexuality, open to blessing or abuse."

"God wants human beings to be faithful to one another in all matters, including sexual ones. Homosexuals, like heterosexuals, are called to either a life of chastity or to a committed relationship with another person."

"I view homosexuality as part of God's creation. The Baptismal Covenant challenges us to seek and serve Christ in all persons and respect the dignity of every human being."

"Homosexual behavior is not a sin in and of itself but to be judged as we judge all of human sexual behavior—as it reflects and expresses God's gracious, merciful, forgiving, unconditional love."

"All of us are sinners seeking a holier way of life. All people should be encouraged to exercise God's gift of sexuality, only in monogamous, lifelong partnerships, regardless of sexual orientation."

Opposition to homosexuality

Those Episcopal Church clergy who see homosexual behavior as sinful had this to say:

"God is unambiguous about this; it is we human beings who seek to justify our own wills over God's will. Neither the argument from genetics nor behavior is particularly convincing. When in doubt, read the instructions. If it's learned behavior, repent and unlearn it. If it's a genetic condition, repent and abstain."

"It is not a greater sin and it too is covered by Jesus' blood."

"It is sin but it can be healed."

"Homosexual actions and thoughts are sins for which we need God's forgiveness. Underlying this is a belief that we need to be changed (redeemed) and made new (sanctified)."

"Homosexual behavior is sinful but it can be healed."

Other views

Some of those who chose the "other" option to the question passed along these thoughts:

"I refuse to be pushed to one extreme or the other."

"The jury is still out. The Bible is very explicit about the role of others based on their gender and orientation but practice has changed in the church. Women were not to teach men, lead or have other roles; similar to the way the Taliban treated women. But that has changed. I believe that if it is proven that homosexuality is a result of natural development, then we need to rethink our traditional teaching."

"I have known good and faithful people who were practicing homosexuals. I have known homosexuals who seemed reckless and engaged in sinful behavior. Lifestyles vary among homosexuals as among heterosexuals."

"The Scriptures are clear about the nature of homosexual acts. They are not considered as part of God's plan. However, God, through Jesus, calls all people to him. If a homosexual person comes to the Altar to be in Communion with God, I trust that God will make the decision who is worthy of that Communion and who is not. My task is to offer God's love, call people to consider their lives and act in conscience, and finally bless people (not their acts) in the Name of Jesus, doing as Jesus did, saying, 'Go and sin no more.' I let the person work out their own salvation. I simply wish to reflect the love of Christ and the joy of Christian living."

Ordination of practicing homosexuals

A follow-up item in my survey to Episcopal Church clergy asked them to respond to this statement: I believe that the ordination of practicing homosexuals in the Episcopal Church (A) is contrary to the clear teachings of Scripture; (B) shows appropriate acceptance of all persons and is right for the church; or (C) other.

Respondents were nearly evenly divided in their answers, with those choosing Option A having a slight edge. Those choosing "A" provided few comments to support their answers. One person wrote: "A person ordained into Holy Orders must be above reproach as much as it is humanly possible. Living in a homosexual relationship is contrary to the teachings of the Church universal, thus such persons should not seek ordination and the Church should not ordain them. I have similar thoughts about divorce."

Another said succinctly: "I believe ordaining practicing homosexuals is divisive to the body of Christ and therefore is wrong."

Another was even more succinct: "Unquestionably!"

Those who chose Option B passed along thoughts like these: "Jesus chose some pretty unlikely people for ministry (prostitutes and tax collectors, among others). However, all clergy should be expected to exercise the gift of sexuality only in lifelong, committed partnerships, whether Holy Matrimony or an equivalent same-sex union."

"A continuation of the justice approach began in our own generation with the full inclusion of women with men and persons of color with white folks (both of which are hard to hide)."

Those who chose Option C provided the most insight into their answers. Here is a sampling of their thoughts.

"I don't believe it is either right or wrong. I am more concerned about the person's standing and relationship before God and his/her calling to serve God. I don't believe that calling is more restricted to homosexual persons than it is to 'straight' women or men."

"I refuse to believe these are the only two options."

"Shows that we stand for the gospel of Jesus Christ against moralism and adherence to the ancient purity codes that God in Christ did away with. But persons, whether heterosexual or homosexual, whose sexual lives are characterized by promiscuity rather than by a faithful relationship are not appropriate candidates for ordination."

"Homosexuals are bound to live up to the same moral strictures incumbent upon heterosexuals."

The response of confessional Lutheranism

The Lutheran Confessions addressed controversies of the time, and since homosexuality was not a disputed matter in the church when the confessions were drafted, it is not surprising to find the confessions silent on homosexuality. What one does find in the confessions is an exposition of Scripture's injunction for sexual chastity. Part of Martin Luther's explanation of the Sixth Commandment in his Large Catechism says, "But because among us there is such a shameful mess and the very dregs of all vice and lewdness, this commandment is directed also against all manner of unchastity, whatever it may be called. . . . In order, therefore, that it may be the more easy in some degree to avoid unchastity, God has commanded the estate of matrimony, that every one may have his proper portion and be satisfied therewith; although God's grace besides is required in order that the heart also may be pure."[80]

Luther was not stating that God's will is that everyone be married. Rather, his words illustrate that it is God's will that sexual relations between people be confined to the marriage bond. Luther's explanation of the Sixth Commandment from his Small Catechism is well known: "We should fear and love God that we lead a pure and decent life in words and actions, and that husband and wife love and honor each other."[81]

The Lutheran Confessions repeat what Holy Scripture says: God commands people to be sexually pure and to confine sexual relations to the holy estate of marriage. Scripture tell us: "Flee from sexual immorality" (1 Corinthians 6:18).

"It is God's will that you should be sanctified: that you should avoid sexual immorality. For God did not call us to be impure, but to live a holy life" (1 Thessalonians 4:3,7).

"Do you not know that the wicked will not inherit the kingdom of God? Do not be deceived: Neither the sexually immoral nor idolaters nor adulterers nor male prostitutes nor homosexual offenders nor thieves nor the greedy nor drunkards nor slanderers nor swindlers will inherit the kingdom of God" (1 Corinthians 6:9,10).

The last passage goes on to say, "And that is what some of you were. But you were washed, you were sanctified, you were justified in the name of the Lord Jesus Christ and by the Spirit of our God" (verse 11). That is one of the responses of confessional Lutheranism regarding homosexual behavior or other sexual impurity: there is forgiveness for those and all sins in the cross of Jesus Christ. Jesus died for the sins of all people. That same Lord looks for people to repent of their sins, trust in him as Savior, and amend their sinful lives. Finally, those whose hearts are filled with Christian faith and repentance enjoy the forgiveness Jesus Christ won for all people.

An end in sight?

The controversy over homosexuality and the ordination of homosexuals as bishops has not subsided in the Episcopal Church. There are those within the Episcopal Church and the Anglican Communion who wonder how long the controversy can continue without repercussions for their church. Time will tell.

There is another controversial issue within the Episcopal Church. This one centers on the unborn, on life itself.

Political action

Episcopalians joined more than one million people, representing 100 religious and religiously-affiliated organizations and congregations, to march on Washington, D.C., April 25 [2004] in support of women's reproductive rights at home and abroad. The march recorded the largest ever crowd count for women's rights in the nation's capital.

The "March for Women's Lives" was co-sponsored by the Religious Coalition for Reproductive Choice (RCRC), an alliance of national organizations from major faith groups, local affiliates, the national Clergy for Choice Network, Spiritual Youth for Reproductive Freedom, and the Black Church Initiative. According to its mission statement, RCRC supports the constitutional right to abortion and solutions to problems such as the spread of HIV/AIDS, inadequate health care and health insurance, and the "severe reduction" in reproductive health care services. The Episcopal Church and the Episcopal Women's Caucus are both members of RCRC.[82]

That information from the Episcopal News Service demonstrates the Episcopal Church's active role in the abortion rights arena. And yet considering the church's wide-ranging opinions on matters of faith and life, one would expect position statements from the church to temper that support for abortion. Those statements abound:

In 1994 the 71st General Convention of the Episcopal Church reaffirmed that all human life is sacred from its inception until death and that all abortion is regarded as having a tragic dimension. "While we acknowledge that in this country it is the legal right of every woman to have a medically safe abortion," the resolution stated, "as Christians we believe strongly that if this right is exercised, it should be used only in extreme situations. We emphatically oppose abortion as a means of birth control, family planning, sex selection, or any reason of mere convenience."[83]

The resolution from the 1994 General Convention also includes these thoughts:

We believe that legislation concerning abortions will not address the root of the problem. We therefore express our deep conviction that any proposed legislation on the part of national or state governments regarding abortions must take special care to see that the individual conscience is respected, and that the responsibility of individuals to reach informed decisions in this matter is acknowledged and honored as the position of the church; and be it further resolved, that this 71st General Convention of the Episcopal Church express its unequivocal opposition to any legislative, executive or judicial action on the part of local, state or national governments that abridge the right of a woman to reach an informed decision about the termination of pregnancy or that would limit the access of a woman to safe means of acting on her decision.[84]

It is clear that the church's position on abortion is consistent with its positions on other matters of faith and life: the church makes statements that touch both sides of the issue and then allows individuals to determine what course of action is in their best interests.

Parish views

So, where do individual Episcopal parishes stand on the issue of abortion? Understandably, one finds various positions. An Episcopal church in Missouri explains: "Abortion is an agonizingly complex issue. We are pro-life and pro-choice. Those seemingly contradictory positions seem to us to be consistent and reasonable. We are pro-life because a fetus is potential human life in a unique way and requires respect and reverence. On the other hand the life and health of a woman is of considerable moral meaning. When those claims for life conflict, women and their husbands and families and physicians are the best people to make moral judgments. The state needs to respect the moral agency of these people. And the Church needs to emphasize the sacred and fragile nature of God's gift of life. We struggle with this issue."[85]

An Episcopal church in the state of Washington maintains: "We oppose any legislative, executive or judicial action limiting decision-making on, or access to abortion. At the same time, we express grave concern about the use of so-called partial birth abortions except in extreme situations. We also oppose abortion simply as a means of birth control. So we might be described as both pro-life and pro-choice. Very Anglican!"[86]

An Episcopal church in New York State explains in one of its booklets:

Because Christianity is a very diverse religion, expressed in many different ways, we often welcome into our church people who have been dissatisfied with their previous religious commitment. Many people turn to the Episcopal Church, and to parishes like St. John's, because we are perceived as having fewer rules and more liberal, inclusive social positions. Some people come to us because their previous church did not celebrate and hold up the ministry of women. Some come to us because their previous church did not welcome gay men and lesbians. Some find us appealing because we have a more tolerant view of abortion, divorce, or other issues of sexuality.

All of this is true: We ordain women, women take prominent places in the life of the church, and, in the Diocese of New York, we have a woman bishop. We have openly gay and lesbian clergy, gay men and lesbians take their places in the life and governance of the church right alongside everyone else, and both single and coupled gay men and lesbians find spiritual nurture here. It is possible for a divorced person to remarry in this church, and the church recognizes and respects the struggle a woman goes through in making decisions about childbirth and pregnancy.[87]

An Episcopal priest in Minnesota stated his views on abortion in one of his sermons:

Episcopalians do not believe in abortion. We BELIEVE that life is sacred . . . that EVERY life is sacred, and a gift from God. Our basic premise is that "when in doubt" protect life. What we allow for is that this is a broken world, and that sometimes, therefore, an abortion can be the lesser of two evils. But notice that language. It is the lesser of two EVILS. We are not saying that it is a positive good, or even neutral. Just that sometimes in life we have to make tough decisions, and that we believe that God and this church understands that . . . and will forgive . . . will welcome and enable us to go on with our lives if we have to go down this road.

I was at the General Convention of the Episcopal Church that passed our resolutions on abortion. They're not law . . . but our "mind of the group" on these matters. What we decided was that we felt it was not the place of government to step too deeply into this most difficult and private of decisions. But at the same time the resolution overtly referred to the sacredness of all human life, abortion being the lesser of two evils, and that it might be appropriate to discuss it with a priest and to seek the sacrament of penance . . . that is, confession and absolution . . . the thing you might do if what you've done is a sin.

From where I sit, that doesn't sound like we believe in abortion . . . but rather that we allow for the possibility in a broken and sinful world."[88]

A divided clergy

It was clear from my survey that Episcopal clergy are divided in their reactions to this statement: I believe that abortion (A) is the taking of human life and therefore wrong; (B) is not wrong, as women have the right to do with their bodies as they choose; or (C) other. Slightly more than half the respondents selected the "A" option, with "C" coming in a close second. Those who chose "A" provided minimal comments:

"Instead of 'wrong' I prefer 'evil' or 'sinful.'"

"Except when necessary to save the life of the mother."

"Unfortunately secularism is the religion of America."

"Abortion is the premeditated murder of unborn children."

"Abortion is wrong, but that does not mean it should be illegal. Morality can't be legislated."

Most of the comments came from those who chose the "other" option. Here is a sampling of their thoughts:

"It is never a 'good' but sometimes the 'right decision' and is a choice. God created us with free will and choice. Otherwise, God never would have put that tree in the garden in the first place. And free will and choice also come with responsibility and consequences."

"Is always wrong but should not be criminalized."

"Abortion is the taking away of the possibility of a human life and as such is highly undesirable, but only the prospective mother has the right to make the decision for or against abortion."

"Abortion is the taking of human life and therefore wrong, but women have the right to do with their bodies as they choose."

"I am politically pro-choice, very strongly, but also fully support the nuanced and careful statements of our General Convention, which talk about the tragic nature of abortion, and agree that general statements are much less helpful than a case by case evaluation."

"I think that women have the right to do what they want, but I personally will miss all those babies."

"I believe that abortion is the taking of a potential life, and is not what God wants of us. I also believe it is a matter to be decided by a woman and whoever she brings into the decision-making process: her doctor, partner, priest, God alone. I do hope that prayer is part of the decision-making process, but also believe that sometimes abortion is the solution that may be best or necessary. I strongly oppose any attempts, either legal or religious, to abridge a woman's right to make this choice."

"Abortion is an evil, but it can be the lesser of two evils."

"Abortion is always a painful choice, even if it is sometimes the most faithful among alternatives."

"Abortion in late pregnancy is not essentially different than infanticide and is thus morally wrong, i.e. something we have a moral obligation not to do. Abortion in early pregnancy does not amount to the killing of a human person and is not contrary to obligation, but in the absence of compelling reasons it is still morally offensive, i.e. something we have morally good reasons to avoid and discourage."

"Abortion is not a good thing (I do not class it as the taking of a human life). But it may be the best of two bad choices, and the woman has the right to choose."

"I am still wrestling with this. For myself, I do not believe I could go through with an abortion. But I am not convicted in such a way that I feel the need to take that right away from other women."

The response of confessional Lutheranism

Abortion is not a new evil in this world. History shows that some ancient civilizations practiced abortion. As with homosexuality, the Lutheran Confessions do not treat the subject of abortion. The confessions are silent on abortion because, just as with homosexuality, there was no controversy in the church regarding abortion. The church was united in its understanding of the Fifth Commandment and the sanctity of life. What the Lutheran Confessions say is that life is to be preserved. Consider these excerpts from Luther's explanation of the Fifth Commandment in his Large Catechism:

Therefore, the entire sum of what it means *not to kill* is to be impressed most explicitly upon the simple-minded. In the first place, that we harm no one, first with our hand or by deed. . . . Secondly, under this commandment not only he is guilty who does evil to his neighbor, but he also who can do him good, prevent, resist evil, defend and save him, so that no bodily harm or hurt happen to him, and yet does not do it. . . . Therefore it is God's ultimate purpose that we suffer harm to befall no man, but show him all good and love."[89]

Again, the Lutheran Confessions expound on biblical statements:

"You [LORD] created my inmost being; you knit me together in my mother's womb" (Psalm 139:13).

"Sons are a heritage from the LORD, children a reward from him" (Psalm 127:3).

"There is no god besides me. I [the LORD] put to death and I bring to life" (Deuteronomy 32:39).

"You shall not murder" (Exodus 20:13).

Strength in division?

Keep in mind that the differences of belief regarding homosexuality and abortion came from Episcopal Church clergy, the teachers of the faith. It should come as no surprise then that the people in the pews have just as varied opinions on abortion, homosexuality, and various other matters. But is this diversity a weakness? Or could it possibly be considered a strength? The answer, according to Anglican thinking, is clear cut.

Review: There are differing opinions in the Episcopal Church on the matter of homosexuality. The ratification of the consecration of an openly gay man to be a bishop sparked controversy in the Anglican Communion. The full ramifications of that incident are yet to be seen.

There is division in the Episcopal Church over the issue of abortion. People on both sides of the issue point to both human reason and Scripture to defend their positions. The church maintains an active role in defending women's legislative rights to have abortions.

6 THE EPISCOPAL CHURCH
and Uniformity

Preview: One of the hallmarks of Anglican thinking is to expect and allow differences of opinion, even in religious matters. Episcopalians refer to this as "the middle road."

Episcopalians are a "both/and" church in an "either/or" world. . . . It is this commitment to "both/and" that makes Episcopalians distinctive. We are both Protestant and Catholic; some Episcopalians are as evangelical as the Baptists, others more Catholic than the Pope. Episcopalians both give primacy to Scripture in matters of faith and find room for the exercise of Reason, as well as for the Tradition of the church. . . . Diversity is possible only for a denomination that has no "confessional writings" stating a single authoritative set of dogmas or doctrines or teachings. Episcopalians have not emphasized static beliefs so much as we have stressed the process of "faith seeking understanding." And the dignity and gift of human reason is nowhere so evident as when the meaning of Scripture turns out to be not so clear as we'd hoped. This has freed Episcopalians to think honestly about the complex demands of human life, whether birth control or abortion, divorce, or blessing same-sex unions.[90]

Invitation to diversity

That statement by an Episcopal Church theologian clearly indicates that various views on matters of faith are welcomed and expected in the Episcopal Church. When one considers the history of the Anglican Church, that it is a "compromise church," that approach is not surprising. And so when people inquire what individual Episcopal parishes stand for, they find information like this:

"The Episcopal Church subscribes to the historic creeds (Nicene Creed and Apostles' Creed). It considers the Bible to be divinely inspired and holds the Eucharist or Lord's Supper to be the central act of Christian worship. However, the Episcopal Church grants great latitude in interpretation of Scripture. It tends to stress less the confession of particular beliefs than the use of *The Book of Common Prayer* in public worship" (an Episcopal church in Pennsylvania).[91]

"Episcopalians hold a range of views, of doctrine convictions, and beliefs. The Episcopal Church grants great latitude in interpretation because the church understands that personal experience and education is an important element of each person's journey of faith. . . . The Episcopal Church is a place where questions and answers are welcome. It has been described as a place that welcomes and encourages 'faith by conversation' and a deepening relationship with God" (an Episcopal church in Florida).[92]

"Our faith is based on the combined foundations of Scripture, tradition and reason. Episcopalians are deeply committed to the unity of God's Church, staying united in our diversity through our shared belief in the reconciling Gospel of Jesus Christ and in the use of the worship services defined by *The Book of Common Prayer*. Because we have traditionally placed more emphasis on the comprehensiveness of God's saving grace than on doctrinal conformity, we both recognize and accept a broad diversity of worship expressions and lifestyles as well as a variety of approaches to faith and commitment" (an Episcopal church in Washington State).[93]

"Disagreement within the Communion is common, acceptable, and even desirable" (an Episcopal church in Virginia).[94]

Those parishes are not speaking out of line. A recent introductory publication by the Episcopal Church makes these statements: "Controversy is often unpleasant, but it is a sign of life; a peaceful church would be one that was slowly dying."[95] And "Anglicans have recognized that almost every important question has a range of possible answers. So they have taken a broad and inclusive approach and been willing to draw on insights from a variety of sources and to accept a both/and approach rather than confront people with an either/or decision."[96]

One Episcopal Church priest, who had been a Lutheran Church—Missouri Synod pastor, made this observation: "Anglicanism encompasses many viewpoints, many theological positions, many personalities and ties them all together into a broad spectrum in one church. There are not a lot of right opinions, or a lot of wrong opinions, just many opinions all tied together."[97]

How far does this kind of thinking go? Consider a TV ad that ran in the San Francisco Bay Area in 2000 and 2002. The screen shows Jesus praying in the Garden of Gethsemane on Thursday of Holy Week. Additional words on the screen say: "Jesus had his doubts, why can't you? Whoever you are, the Episcopal Church welcomes you."[98]

Survey results

In view of statements like these, asking Episcopal Church clergy how they view diversity of thought and belief did not produce unexpected results. Respondents were asked to indicate how they would complete this statement: It is ____ that the members of my parish agree in matters of faith and doctrine. The choices were (A) not important at all; (B) somewhat important; (C) important; and (D) very important.

Those who chose the "A" option included thoughts like these: "The Anglican church was founded as a compromise between Protestants and Catholics in England. Complete agreement on doctrine has never been part of our tradition in 500 years."

"Not important but helpful."

"Absolutely not. Let's get together and worship God."

A priest who selected the "B. somewhat important" option wrote, "All I ask of my parishioners is that they agree to the Outline of Faith as listed in *The Book of Common Prayer*. I ask also that they are obedient to the teachings of *The Book of Common Prayer* as they are expressed in the liturgy and the supporting rubric. I teach that *The Book of Common Prayer* is based entirely on Scripture and the liturgy finds its origins in Scripture, therefore, to adhere to the principles as expressed in *The Book of Common Prayer* is Scripturally sound and good doctrine. However, the point of the Anglican teachings is to allow the individual Christian to discover the teachings of the Church and apply them on their own. That means we have doctrine but are not doctrinaire and we have a dogma but we are not dogmatic."

Some of those who selected the "C. important" option mentioned this:

"It is important, but 'the way we do church' is insignificant compared to understanding why God created us (for his glory), his purpose for us (eternal life with the Godhead), and our way into full communion with the Godhead (through Jesus Christ our Lord)."

"Not necessarily homogeneity of views. Each person has a right and responsibility for their own choices and, while doctrinal unity is important, we must be careful to separate certain doctrinal matters from the essentials of salvation, through which we are united in Christ (even with some who otherwise disagree with us)."

Some of those who said it was "very important" for the members of their parish to agree in matters of faith and doctrine said this:

"It is very important, but new Christians must be taught this."

"It depends if they all agree on what is true. If they all agreed on falsehood, that would not be useful."

While this question did not include an "other" option, several respondents created one and provided this rationale: "I doubt that the members of my church care to agree on matters of faith and doctrine. We really struggle with relativism. Church members don't seem to care very much about these issues, except as they relate to homosexuality at the moment. When we argue, I refer to the Bible and *The Book of Common Prayer*, but they may or may not find them compelling, and seem to have little energy for solving anything."

"What's important is not that they agree, but that they share a core commitment to Jesus Christ and a desire to know him by way of the study of the Bible and to worship him by means of *The Book of Common Prayer*."

"The Gospel gives us a capacity for ambiguity. We need to be able to put it into our own words. I really believe that to be the Anglican way."

The *via media*

These responses and previous survey responses cited in earlier chapters all exemplify what one Episcopalian priest stated about his church on his parish's Web site: "We are flexible spiritually. We love and follow the Anglican *via media,* 'middle way.' Where other traditions rely on confessional statements or their hierarchy to set boundaries and rules, the Anglican tradition has always tried to be a big tent with room for all. The *via media* emphasizes a preference for including rather than excluding, tolerance rather than dogmatism, feminine more than the masculine, the poetic rather than the systematic."[99]

One Episcopalian author even went so far as to say, "For the Anglican, given a choice between heresy and schism, we see schism as the greater sin."[100] Clergy who were given an opportunity to react to that statement agreed with it.

I was aware of the Episcopal Church's preference for the *via media* before sending out my survey. That is why options for answering the questions and completing the statements were far-ranging and, with the exception of one question, included an "other" option. In spite of that accommodation, there were still some respondents who were uncomfortable with the options provided for answering the questions.

"I began this questionnaire and then discovered that the either/or choices don't suit me very well. Very Anglican of me, don't you think?"

"We tend to both . . . and solutions."

"Where is the middle way?"

The Lutheran Confessions on unity and uniformity

The dictionary definition of *uniformity* is, predictably, "the quality or state of being uniform."[101] One of the definitions of *uniform* is "consistent in conduct or opinion."[102] The Lutheran Confessions do distinguish between uniformity and unity. In the confessions there is no insistence that Lutheran churches be completely uniform in their rites and customs. Where God has not spoken, the confessions recognize that Christian freedom exists. And yet the confessions point out the importance of preserving the unity of the faith.

The Thorough Declaration of the Formula of Concord states: From this our explanation, friends and enemies, and therefore every one, may clearly infer that we have no intention of yielding aught of the eternal, immutable truth of God for the sake of temporal peace, tranquility, and unity (which, moreover, is not in our power to do). Nor would such peace and unity, since it is devised against the truth and for its suppression, have any permanency. Still less are we inclined to adorn and conceal a corruption of the pure doctrine and manifest, condemned errors. But we entertain heartfelt pleasure and love for, and are on our part sincerely inclined and anxious to advance, that unity according to our utmost power, by which His glory remains to God uninjured, nothing of the divine truth of the Holy Gospel is surrendered, no room is given to the least error, poor sinners are brought to true, genuine repentance, raised up by faith, confirmed in new obedience, and thus justified and eternally saved alone through the sole merit of Christ.[103]

Again the confessions articulate what the Scriptures say: "I appeal to you, brothers, in the name of our Lord Jesus Christ, that all of you agree with one another so that there may be no divisions among you and that you may be perfectly united in mind and thought" (1 Corinthians 1:10).

"Make every effort to keep the unity of the Spirit through the bond of peace" (Ephesians 4:3).

"Let the peace of Christ rule in your hearts, since as members of one body you were called to peace" (Colossians 3:15).

"How good and pleasant it is when brothers live together in unity!" (Psalm 133:1).

"Watch your life and doctrine closely" (1 Timothy 4:16).

Diversity and ecumenism

When one examines the Episcopal Church and sees such allowances for different beliefs and a general lack of concern for uniformity, one might think that the Episcopal Church would display such an ecumenical spirit that it would join forces with any and every church that calls itself Christian. That is not the case, however. This is one area where the church tries to remove ambiguity and draw the line.

Review: Apart from the teachings of the Nicene Creed, the Apostles' Creed, and *The Book of Common Prayer* in general, the Episcopal Church does not look for uniformity in belief from its members. This approach is consistent with what the church is—a church not guided by confessions. The Episcopal Church views that lack of uniformity as a strength.

7 THE EPISCOPAL CHURCH
and Other Churches

Preview: The Episcopal Church enjoys a close relationship with the other 37 churches of the Anglican Communion. In addition, the church enjoys close ties with some churches outside the Anglican Communion and maintains dialogues with other churches in the hope of expressing a unity of some kind.

Previous chapters have described the Episcopal Church's membership in the Anglican Communion. That Communion involves a large, diverse group of people who find common ground in a few basic beliefs, forms of worship, and an organizational structure that invites cooperation.

Additionally, the Episcopal Church seeks to establish close relations with church bodies outside the Anglican Communion. In fact, the church has an agency that oversees this work: the Office of Ecumenical and Interfaith Relations. That office "is charged with fostering unity among the separated branches of the Christian church, for the sake of cooperation and mission in the world."[104]

What constitutes unity?

After reading the previous chapter, you might be wondering on what basis the Episcopal Church would express unity with other churches when unity within the church is not an issue for many. Officially, the Episcopal Church sees four items that are essential for unity. These items come from what is called the Chicago-Lambeth Quadrilateral, a meeting of the church's bishops that took place in Chicago, Illinois, in 1886. It saw agreement on these items as essential for unity:

1. The Holy Scriptures of the Old and New Testament as the revealed Word of God.
2. The Nicene Creed as the sufficient statement of the Christian Faith.
3. The two Sacraments—Baptism and the Supper of the Lord—ministered with unfailing use of Christ's words of institution and of the elements ordained by Him.
4. The Historic Episcopate, locally adapted in the methods of its administration to the varying needs of the nations and peoples called of God into the unity of His Church.[105]

To many Episcopalians, agreement on these four items is essential if their church is to unite with another church in any formal way. References to these items will surface later in clergy responses to my survey.

Churches Uniting in Christ

The result of the Episcopal Church's desire to unite with other church bodies has been successful. The Episcopal Church is a member of Churches Uniting in Christ, an association of "nine Christian communions that have pledged to live more closely together in expressing their unity in Christ and to combat racism together."[106] The Churches Uniting in Christ are the African Methodist Episcopal Church, the African Methodist Episcopal Zion Church, the Christian Church (Disciples of Christ), Christian Methodist Episcopal Church, the Episcopal Church of the United States, the International Council of Community Churches, the Presbyterian Church (USA), the United Church of Christ, and the United Methodist Church.

Dialogue with other churches

The Episcopal Church is in various stages of dialogue with several other church bodies, including the Orthodox Church, the Roman Catholic Church, and the Moravian Church. In some cases, the dialogues have been taking place for many years. In other cases, the dialogues have begun fairly recently. In all cases, the dialogues have the purpose of better understanding the faith, traditions, and ministries of other churches, and exploring ways of how churches might have closer relationships with one another.

"Full Communion"

For the Episcopal Church, the ultimate fruit of dialogue with other churches is "full Communion." The Episcopal Church describes full Communion as follows:

1. Each Communion [church] recognizes the catholicity and independence of the other and maintains its own.
2. Each Communion agrees to admit members of the other Communion to participate in the Sacraments.
3. Intercommunion does not require from either Communion the acceptance of all doctrinal opinion, sacramental devotion, or liturgical practice characteristic of the other but implies that each believes the other to hold all the essentials of the Christian faith.[107]

Full Communion is not a merger of churches. Confessional Lutherans might understand the concept of full Communion in terms of "being in fellowship" with another church body. Full Communion does enable clergy from one church to cross over and serve in the other church. Full Communion also provides for mutual cooperation and coordinated ministries.

The Episcopal Church is in full Communion with all the churches of the Anglican Communion, as well as the Old Catholic Churches of Europe, the united churches of the Indian subcontinent, the Mar Thoma Church (India), and the Philippine Independent Church.[108] Recently, the Episcopal Church's list of full Communion partners increased by one.

The Evangelical Lutheran Church in America

In January 2001 the Episcopal Church and the Evangelical Lutheran Church in America (ELCA) formally entered into full Communion with each another. This action was the result of 30 years of dialogue. Each church, through its organizational structures, approved a *Concordat of Agreement.* The agreement declares that each church recognizes the other as holding "all the essentials of the Christian faith, although this does not require from either church acceptance of all doctrinal formulations of the other."[109] While that statement is consistent with Anglican thinking, it certainly is foreign to confessional Lutheranism. Confessional Lutherans understand that churches can cooperate in ministries and share joint worship, Communion, and prayer only after there is agreement in doctrinal matters.

The Evangelical Lutheran Church in America understands its full Communion with the Episcopal Church in these six ways:

[There is now] (1) a common confession of the Christian faith; (2) a mutual recognition of Baptism and the Lord's Supper, allowing for joint worship and an exchangeability of members; (3) a mutual recognition and availability of ministers; (4) a common commitment to evangelism, witness and service; (5) a means of common decision making on critical common issues of faith and life; and (6) a mutual lifting of any condemnations that exist between the churches.[110]

Full Communion between the Episcopal Church and ELCA does not mean that each church automatically participates in the full Communion of the other church. For instance, by means of the *Concordat* the Evangelical Lutheran Church in America is not in full Communion with the churches of the entire Anglican Communion. Nor is the Episcopal Church in full Communion with the member churches of the Lutheran World Federation, the Presbyterian Church (USA), the Reformed Church in America and the United Church of Christ, as the ELCA is.[111] Confessional Lutherans would recognize this arrangement as "triangular fellowship," whereby one church is in fellowship with a second but not with the churches that are in fellowship with the second.

Membership in other organizations
In addition to the full Communion partners that it enjoys, the Episcopal Church cooperates with other churches by virtue of

its membership in the National Council of Churches in Christ. This is an association of 36 churches in the United States. Moreover, the Episcopal Church belongs to the World Council of Churches, which claims 340 member churches throughout the world.

In March 2005, the *Episcopal News Service* announced:

A new ecumenical organization known as Christian Churches Together in the United States of America (CCT-USA) will be launched in June 1-3, 2005. . . . The Episcopal Church has been involved in discussion for several years, with the National Council of Churches and others, about how to 'broaden the ecumenical table' in the US, bringing together Roman Catholics, Orthodox, mainline Protestants, primarily ethnic churches, Evangelicals and Pentecostals in a new forum for prayer, dialogue, and action. . . .

Full members [of CCT-USA] now include the Evangelical Lutheran Church in America, the Church of God, the Christian Church (Disciples of Christ), the Cooperative Baptist Fellowship (CBF), the United Methodist Church, several Orthodox bodies, the Salvation Army, the United Church of Christ, Open Bible Churches, the International Pentecostal Holiness Church, Evangelicals for Social Action, World Vision, and a number of others.[112]

The Episcopal Church, then, is in every way an ecumenical church, a church that joins together with other Christian churches in worship and ministry even when there is not complete agreement in belief. That should not come as a surprise, for we have seen that the lack of complete agreement in belief is not expected or required even within the Episcopal Church.

Survey results

So where do Episcopal clergy stand on the subject of their church and other churches? The last question in my survey invited participants to respond to this statement: As a leader in the Episcopal Church, I believe that full Communion with other Christian churches should be made on the basis of (A) agreement in the essential matters of the Christian faith; (B) agreement in all parts of the Christian faith; (C) simply acknowledging that Jesus Christ is the Son of God and the Savior of the world; or (D) other. While the results were expectedly varied, the overwhelming choice was "A," while "B" received the very weakest support. Here is a sampling of clergy responses:

"While I respect the faith of other Christian communities, I believe that I am in Communion with other Christians when they agree to the following: (1) The Scriptures are the inspired word of God and contain all that is necessary for salvation; (2) the Apostles' and Nicene Creeds are complete and adequate statements of faith; (3) the two Sacraments were ordained by Christ himself and are administered with Christ's words and the elements used by him; and (4) the Historic Episcopate (are in the historic line of Apostolic succession)."

"We can all work together to spread the Gospel without being in full communion. Oneness in unity and purpose does not have to mean we all believe the small details."

"There are degrees of communion. The level of communion is predicated by agreement in faith, doctrine, and practice. My parish is not in fellowship with the head of ECUSA and those who participated in the consecration of Gene Robinson. All Episcopalian clergy are not free to take part in presiding at worship at our parish. We require some commonality of faith, doctrine, and practice of Christianity. We in fact have a higher degree of communion with some other denominations or churches than within the Episcopal Church."

"D. Certainly not A or B, but even C does not fully grasp the transformative nature of the act of receiving communion together. Communion not only reflects community, it creates it."

"'One Lord, One Faith, One Baptism, One God and Father of us all.' This is the basis of Christian union, but the desire to be together or to remain together has remained out of our reach. Truth scattered along the lines of doctrine, and has not found its way back yet. I am sure that when it does, it will look a lot like love."

"Agreement in the essential matters of the Christian faith, that being Christ's atonement for us and the sacraments of Baptism and Holy Communion. With regard to the latter, whether we imagine communion as transubstantiation, consubstantiation, or simply a memorial is not a deciding issue. It is a mystery (hence 'sacrament') through which God gives us grace."

The majority of respondents to the survey agreed with the official position of their church when they indicated that there needs to be agreement in the essential matters of the Christian faith before churches can enter into full Communion.

Confessional Lutheranism

How does that compare with confessional Lutheranism? *This We Believe* states:

We believe that God directs believers to acknowledge oneness in faith with Christians whose confession of faith submits to all the teachings of Scripture (John 8:31; 1 Thessalonians 5:21,22). We believe, furthermore, that individuals through their membership in a church body commit themselves to the doctrine and practice of that church. To assert that unity exists where there is no agreement in confession is to presume to look into people's hearts. Only God can look into people's hearts. It is not necessary that all Christians agree on matters of church ritual or organization. About these the New Testament gives no commands (Romans 14:17).[113]

And repeating a section from that confessional statement that had been offered earlier:

God directs believers not to practice religious fellowship with those whose confession and actions reveal that they teach, tolerate, support, or defend error (2 John 10,11). When error appears in the church, Christians will try to preserve their fellowship by patiently admonishing the offenders, in the hope that they will turn from their error (2 Timothy 2:25,26; Titus 3:10). But the Lord commands believers not to practice church fellowship with people who persist in teaching or adhering to beliefs that are false (Romans 16:17,18).[114]

One-on-one conversations

Reading what clergy have written in response to survey questions gives one a good feel for what they think and believe, but there is no substitute for sitting down and conversing with church leaders. This will become clear in the next chapter.

Review: The Episcopal Church enjoys being in full Communion with the other churches of the Anglican Communion. Recently, the church entered into full Communion with the Evangelical Lutheran Church in America. The Episcopal Church belongs to various ecumenical organizations. Clergy are divided over how much agreement in faith needs to be in place before their church can enter into full Communion with other churches.

INTERVIEWS WITH AN EPISCOPALIAN BISHOP, A PRIEST, *and the Presiding Bishop*

Preview: An Episcopalian bishop, a priest, and the Presiding Bishop provide candid responses to a variety of questions.

Rev. James L. Jelinek was consecrated as the eighth bishop of the Minnesota Diocese on October 29, 1993. As bishop, Jelinek supervises the 110 Episcopal parishes in his diocese. That supervisory work includes, among other duties, making periodic visits to all 110 congregations, assisting parishes to fill vacancies in the offices of priest and deacon, and officiating at the congregations' confirmations. On a beautiful fall afternoon in 2004, Bishop Jelinek sat down with me to explain his faith and work.

Jelinek is an Episcopal Church bishop, but he has a Lutheran background. He grew up in Milwaukee, Wisconsin. He belonged to a congregation that was part of the Lutheran Church in America (LCA), a church body that later merged with the American Lutheran Church (ALC) and the Association of Evangelical Lutheran Churches (AELC) to form the Evangelical Lutheran Church in America (ELCA). He recalled being involved in his church from early on. His father at one time was president of the church council.

In his youth, Jelinek was involved in his church, but he sensed there was something wrong with his church. He heard plenty of law from the pulpit but not much gospel. In fact, his impression of God at that time was that he was a "celestial sniper," hunting and shooting down people with his law but not healing the wounded with his gospel. Further disillusionment came when Jelinek was confirmed in the Lutheran faith. After completing confirmation class and being readied to receive Holy Communion, he saw with sadness how infrequently his congregation offered the sacrament. He wondered why the sacrament was not offered more often if it was that important.

Years later Jelinek graduated from Carthage College, a Lutheran college that was then located in Carthage, Illinois. During his senior year at Carthage, Jelinek attended a worship service at the local Episcopal church. At that church he perceived that "God is primarily merciful, as opposed to the law message I perceived in the Lutheran church." Jelinek made similar statements in a sermon preached on November 16, 2003. "At my first Eucharist in the Episcopal Church we prayed a lovely prayer called 'The Prayer of Humble Access,' in which God is described as one 'whose property is always to have mercy.' I was stunned. I was overjoyed that a whole people, these Episcopalians, thought that the primary dimension of God is to have mercy."[115] In addition, his perception was that in the Episcopal Church, God was "for" certain things, while in the Lutheran church, God was "against" certain things.

At this point Jelinek knew that he could not continue in the Lutheran church. He believed his options were to join either the Roman Catholic Church or the Episcopal Church. The influence of a college roommate swayed him to join the Episcopal Church.

While attending graduate school in Nashville, Tennessee, Jelinek attended the worship services of an Episcopal parish. He was influenced positively by the parish's priest, to the degree that he considered entering the priesthood, which he did. Jelinek then served as a parish priest for 22 years in Tennessee, Ohio, and California. In 1993, Jelinek was elected as the eighth bishop of the Minnesota diocese.

Valuing diversity

In my interview with Bishop Jelinek, I asked whether it was accurate to say that the Episcopal Church values the diversity of people's beliefs. The bishop gave a qualifying yes to that question. The issue, in his opinion, is that there is a difference between dogma and doctrine. "There are two dogmas in the Episcopal Church: one is the Trinity, the other is the hypostatic union of God and man in Jesus Christ. We expect the clergy to believe these things. Then there are doctrines: the virgin birth, the ascension of Christ, premarital sex, the ordination of women. We aren't as unified there."

According to Jelinek, part of the reason for the lack of unity can be attributed to people's understanding of the Bible. He said there are difficulties when "people look at what the Holy Spirit was doing at one time in history and then try to make that the rule for all time." He cited the ordination of women as an example. In his thinking, while the church in the 1st century might have heard the Holy Spirit forbidding the ordination of women, the church of the 21st century is to be allowed the opportunity to hear the Holy Spirit speaking differently, allowing the ordination of women. However, he added, there is diversity when some people in the 21st century hold to 1st-century beliefs.

Strengths of the church

When asked to list the strengths of the Episcopal Church, Bishop Jelinek quickly provided four. The first is the Incarnation of Jesus Christ. "It is most critical to us. It influences and shapes us predominately. Incarnation happens in everyone. God indwells everyone." His observation was that the Episcopal Church is going faster than other churches in seeing and serving the Christ in everyone, and that is why the church is having turmoil.

A second strength mentioned was liturgical tradition. "We take the liturgy so seriously that we joke about it!" He spoke of the unifying effect of *The Book of Common Prayer,* enabling Episcopalians to feel at home, no matter where they might be worshiping.

A third strength listed was diversity of culture. Jelinek noted that the bishop of New York told him recently that the Eucharist is being celebrated in 13 different languages in the Episcopal Church. Jelinek stated that in his own diocese, worship services were being conducted in four different languages. And, he says, there is something beneficial from that multicultural dimension: "Diversity keeps us from thinking we are the best."

A fourth strength was the size of the congregations. "Our churches are of sizes that feel like a community to the people who are in them." Because they are on the small size, he said he can get a feel for their "soul" when he visits them.

Dealing with controversy

Bishop Jelinek was the host bishop at the 2003 General Convention, where the ratification of the consecration of Bishop V. Gene Robinson, an openly gay man, took place. Shortly after the convention, Jelinek made these statements: "This past week, when the leaders of the Episcopal Church spoke, it became very clear that a great number among us believe that the Holy Spirit has pushed or called us to speak differently about homosexual persons, homosexuality, and homosexual acts. The Holy Spirit has led us to recognize with honesty that homosexuality can indeed be a wholesome example to God's people, that homosexuality is itself morally neutral, and that homosexual behaviors are subject to the same moral judgments as are heterosexual behaviors. . . . By our actions in the work of the General Convention, I believe that we have made it evermore clear that all are welcome in the Episcopal Church, even those who are not yet members. We have asked no one to leave and my prayer remains that no one will leave. On the other hand, we have sent a strong message to the Diocese of Minnesota, the Episcopal Church in the United States, and, in fact, the world, that gay and lesbian people are welcome in the Episcopal Church. I am proud of our Church! Come join us! I also understand that some of our sisters and brothers will be unhappy, dismayed, and shocked at the action of the General Convention. There continues to be room for all in the Episcopal Church and I remain convinced that we can and will continue to embrace and welcome the diversity and ambiguity of this decision. We have a history of doing that for over two hundred years. Indeed, the Church has been shaken this week. It was shaken when the Church acted to change its views of slavery, and it was shaken when the church acted to change its views on the role of women."[116]

When asked about the continuing ramifications of the 2003 General Convention's actions, Jelinek noted that the difficulty with the Robinson case is that there is no structure to watch over independent churches that are part of the Anglican Communion. He said, "We could not have imagined the hurt of our actions, and we are sorry for that. We are working hard for reconciliation and non-schism."

View toward other Lutherans

Because the Evangelical Lutheran Church in America (ELCA) entered into an agreement of full Communion with the Episcopal Church, Jelinek is familiar with that branch of Lutheranism. I was curious about his awareness of other Lutheran church bodies, such as the Wisconsin Evangelical Lutheran Synod (WELS) and The Lutheran Church—Missouri Synod (LCMS). With a smile and a twinkle in his eye, he said: "Because you keep yourselves apart, we don't know enough about you to be prejudiced!" Noting the differences that separate the Episcopal Church from other Lutheran church bodies, he noted: "If you hear God speaking to you in another way, you will change." But even if the kinds of changes he is looking for do not take place, he observed that "the gift of religions, denominations, is that everyone has the possibility of hearing God's Word."

Perception by other Lutherans

As a follow up to the previous question, I asked, "What would you want Lutherans who are not part of the ELCA-Episcopal Church full Communion agreement to know better about the Episcopal Church?" Jelinek had three responses:

"We too are disciples of Christ and believe that we are living as we are moved by the Holy Spirit.

"In our understanding, the danger of a literal reading of Scriptures could be a freezing of God in time and a denial of the Holy Spirit to move humanity.

"I don't like it when people say about things in the Bible, 'It's *only* a myth.' The Bible has myths. But a myth characterizes something profound about the nature of God, humans and their relations with God and one another. Myths are true, whether they are historical or not."

Interview with a priest

At the time of this writing, Rev. Paul Rider was the priest-in-charge at St. John Episcopal Church in Mankato, Minnesota. As priest-in-charge, Rider was appointed by Bishop James Jelinek to serve the parish until it calls a regular priest. On a crisp day in November 2004, Rev. Rider shared with me his thoughts on being an Episcopalian and a priest in the Episcopal Church.

Rev. Rider describes himself as a "cradle Episcopalian," one who grew up in the Episcopal Church. He graduated from Nashotah House Theological Seminary in Nashotah, Wisconsin. Prior to his present work in Minnesota, he served parishes in Texas and North Dakota.

In my interview with Rev. Rider, I asked questions similar to the ones I posed to Bishop Jelinek.

Valuing diversity, again

When asked whether it was accurate to say that the Episcopal Church values the diversity of people's beliefs, Rider replied: "It depends on what you mean by people's beliefs. It is generally true. You can find some progressive churches where almost anything goes. There is no litmus test, but it's getting to be that way in some dioceses and congregations regarding practices. The Lambeth Quadrilateral contains the items that are essential for faith. There is room for diversity beyond that."

As a follow-up question, I asked, "If diversity of belief is welcomed in the Episcopal Church, does there come a time when uniformity of doctrine is sought or welcomed? If so, when is that?"

Rider answered: "*Uniformity* is not a word we are comfortable with." He explained that *unity* rather than *uniformity* would better describe his position as an Episcopalian. And he saw mechanisms in place to foster unity. "We are a church that does see the bishops as the central point of unity within the body. The bishop holds the diocese together. The conventions of each diocese also address unity. The actions of the General Convention are another method by which we try to achieve unity." Regarding his personal experience with unity, Rider explained: "I'll always be obedient to my bishop." He went on to say that he changed locations in his ministry when obedience to a former bishop became too challenging.

Strengths of the church

When asked to outline the strengths of the Episcopal Church, Rider spoke of three areas. The first was Anglicanism in general. "Anglicanism provides the ability to have a broad umbrella under which diversity of thought is allowed to flourish. You have differences of opinions on the Eucharist, worship and practice. We have been able to hold that in tension, but I fear it is breaking up."

A second strength listed was social ministry and outreach. Rider explained that in the minds of some, the Episcopal Church got into trouble in the 1960s. "Some of our people moved south to participate in the Civil Rights movement. We got involved in serving the homeless and offering meal programs. We were opposed to the Vietnam War." But, he noted, "criticism [of that sort of thing] is going by the wayside." He sees the church's continuing involvement in social issues as a strength because people are being led to see social issues as religious issues.

A third strength was the recognition of the diversity of gifts among all people in the church. He noted that "we have been perceived as being top-down in the church. But in the Catechism, laypeople are mentioned first."

Dealing with controversy

When asked about the recent controversy in the church regarding the consecration of a gay bishop, Rider said that "the Episcopal Church is not going to turn back the clock. The Episcopal Church will go forward." He did see the issue as part of a larger picture: "It's the struggle of traditional values over against nontraditional values." And, he noted, "It is very sad that the church might split over this."

Perception by other Lutherans

When asked what he would want people who belonged to WELS and LCMS to know better about the Episcopal Church, Rider replied: "The Episcopal Church has a high view of Scripture. Other churches have a more literalistic view of Scripture. It is the church's responsibility to interpret through the Scripture how God is moving and working among us and what he's calling us to do. An understanding of Scripture might change. God does not change, but society does."

Interview with the Presiding Bishop

On June 18, 2006, the delegates to the General Convention of the Episcopal Church made history. They elected the first woman to the office of Presiding Bishop in their church. Their choice was Rev. Katharine Jefferts Schori. Her ascendancy to the top position in the Episcopal Church is a remarkable one, considering that she did not become a priest until 1994. Through an e-mail interview, Bishop Jefferts Schori provided the following information.

Background

Like many of those under her leadership, Bishop Jefferts Schori came to the Episcopal Church from another church. Her mother was Roman Catholic, and her father had been raised in the Methodist church. Jefferts Schori was raised in the Roman Catholic Church, even attending an all-girl convent school until fifth grade. When she and her parents moved across the country, they left Roman Catholicism and joined the Episcopal Church.

Bishop Jefferts Schori's first career was in oceanography. As a result of positive feedback received from serving as a substitute preacher on a Sunday morning, she began thinking of training for the priesthood. She was ordained in 1994 and elected bishop of the Diocese of Nevada in 2000. In my interview with the Presiding Bishop, I asked questions similar to those I had posed to other Episcopal Church clergy.

Valuing diversity, once more

Does the Episcopal Church value the diversity of people's beliefs? It was no surprise to receive the answer: "Anglicanism has always held as a high value the ability to be a broad tent. The Elizabethan Settlement was a formal way of asserting this—a broad variety of theologies and liturgical styles were to be tolerated and accepted. At our best, this is who we are—living in tension with those who disagree. . . . We may be a messy lot, but we think that a blessing most of the time, as we seek to live out the call God gives us—in this and every age."

When asked if there are core beliefs that are absolutely essential for an Episcopalian to uphold, the Presiding Bishop responded: "We are a pretty classic case of *lex orandi, lex credendi.*" Literally, the expression means "the law of prayer is the law of belief." It is an expression that says that worship reflects one's theology.

Bishop Jefferts Schori continued: "*The Book of Common Prayer* is the best summary of our theology. The 'Outline of the Faith' or 'Catechism' in its latter pages is a reasonable summary of how we approach a number of central issues and questions. Ecumenically, the Chicago-Lambeth Quadrilateral sums up what is essential for us: the Scriptures of Old and New Testaments, the Nicene Creed, the two dominical sacraments, and the historic episcopate as locally adapted."

Dealing with controversy

When the 75th General Convention of the Episcopal Church met in Columbus, Ohio, in June 2006, there were expectations that the church would address current controversies, such as the consecration of a gay bishop. As it turned out, the convention created more controversy by electing for the first time a woman to the office of Presiding Bishop. Jefferts Schori is well aware of the controversy but tries to keep it in perspective: "There are three diocesan bishops (of 150 or so active bishops) who opposed the ordination of women and, thus, my election. One of them has recently encouraged his diocese to formally leave the Episcopal Church. The opposition is small in number, albeit quite vocal. There is greater opposition to parts of the church, and to leaders in the church, who advocate for inclusivity and a more generous interpretation of Scripture, and that pattern is of long standing. While we have historically been a broad and inclusive church and communion, there is some indication that a small percentage of the members of this church have lost patience with the direction in which the majority is moving. That is an ancient pattern, but the reactivity and impatience of the times make it more difficult to maintain the tension."

What about the controversy with other churches in the Anglican Communion? Could the Episcopal Church not be welcome someday in the Anglican Communion? Bishop Jefferts Schori: "The Episcopal Church, as a child of the Church of England, was the first partner in the Anglican Communion. I think it unlikely that the Communion as a whole would reject our membership. I do think it possible, however, that more conservative elements in the Communion may choose to walk a divergent path. In terms of the issues of homosexuality, the Episcopal Church is only the 'identified patient.' These issues are of concern in many, many other parts of the Communion, we are not alone in having acted to broaden our inclusivity, and we are not alone in our public positions. At least some of the current difficulty across the Communion has to do with understandable attitudes toward the United States and its government's policies. For example, the relatively minor reaction to the blessing of same-gender unions in Canada, and in England (where they are far more numerous than in the United States), is, I believe, a result of that conflation in some people's minds."

View of Lutherans

What impressions does the Presiding Bishop have of the Lutheran heritage? "Not unlike the Anglican, with some of the same challenges in terms of the world seeing us both as 'the frozen chosen.' The Lutheran tradition has a fine and honored catechetical tradition, and an attention to detail, structure, and process that can be a robust gift."

Review: A bishop, a priest, and the Presiding Bishop of the Episcopal Church answer questions that were posed to them. All individuals reiterate thoughts and opinions that other clergy members have expressed in my survey.

MEETING INDIVIDUAL *Episcopalians*

Preview: A group of lay members from an Episcopal parish explain their faith and life experiences.

Surveying clergy and interviewing an Episcopalian bishop, a priest, and the Presiding Bishop provided insight on the views and beliefs of some of the clergy in the church, but what are the people in the pews thinking? A focus group conducted at St. Mark Episcopal Church in Mankato, Minnesota, gave some initial answers to that question.

A dozen members of the congregation, ranging in age from 15 to 83, answered questions and freely offered their thoughts on being Episcopalians. The members present represented a broad spectrum of the parish. Five of the individuals described themselves as lifelong Episcopalians, while the remaining seven had joined the church later in life for various reasons. Of the latter group, one had been raised in the Methodist church, another in the Roman Catholic Church, still another in the United Church of Christ, and others in The Lutheran Church—Missouri Synod and the predecessor church bodies that form the Evangelical Lutheran Church in America.

Reasons for joining

Those who joined the Episcopal Church as adults explained what influenced their decisions. A husband and wife that had Roman Catholic and Lutheran backgrounds found it easier to join a new church when they relocated to a different part of the country. For them, the Episcopal Church was a compromise church. Three other women spoke of changing their membership to join their husbands in the Episcopal Church. A university professor who grew up in the Roman Catholic Church joined the Episcopal Church after relocating and becoming friends with the local Episcopal Church rector. Besides, he added, there were "hierarchical issues" with the Roman Catholic Church that influenced his decision to change churches. Those who joined the Episcopal Church as adults commented on the friendly, inviting atmosphere of the parishes they visited.

Reasons for remaining

All members of the focus group were asked, "What two factors are instrumental for you in remaining a member of the Episcopal Church?"

A middle-aged woman remarked that in her opinion, "The Episcopal Church is more accepting of all people." Another middle-aged woman said, "One factor has been because of a strong message from the church regarding social consciousness and social change. Another reason has been because of the wonderful, selfless, talented people I have encountered—priests, congregation members and diocesan representatives." A middle-aged man said, "I like the liturgy. I'm comfortable with it. Church is a family for me. It's small enough that you can get to know people."

An elderly man was very frank when he said that "the church has constantly disappointed me because of the changes they have made," but then he freely admitted that he was "too lazy" to make a change at this point in his life. He said, "I had to go outside my church to learn what I needed to know." He explained that while he retained his membership in his Episcopal church, he attended a Baptist church "to be born again." While the church has disappointed him, he said he was comfortable in the church. And, he added, "I can't go to sleep during my priest's sermons."

A woman who had been raised a Roman Catholic said that she remained a member of the Episcopal Church in spite of all the changes in the church she didn't agree with. But, she added, she did not want to start over and find another church. She wanted to stay with what is familiar.

The 15-year-old in the group said she remained a member of the church because she did not have a choice but added in all seriousness that she liked the church's desire to change as society changed. In fact, she did not want the church to remain the same.

Views toward the Bible

The next question I asked was "What is your understanding of your church's teaching that God inspired the writers of the Bible? Do 'inspired' and 'inerrant' go together?"

The elderly gentleman who spoke of having to go outside his church to learn what he needed to know, stated that he believed the Bible "is God's holy word—absolute truth and not to be tampered with."

A woman with a Roman Catholic background said that since the Bible was written so long ago, we need to look at it differently in our culture.

A middle-aged woman with a previous Lutheran background pointed out that she would "not at all agree that inspired and inerrant go together." She went on to say, "Although I am not a student of Episcopalian theology, my understanding of our church's position on the writers of the Bible is that they were humans inspired by God. My own beliefs are that those very human writers of the Bible were not omniscient and frequently translations can turn a passage on its head."

A well-educated gentleman stated that "early books in the Old Testament are not to be taken literally." And yet he said that does not mean that those books are meaningless, because "all parts of the Bible point to important lessons to learn about ourselves and others."

Change in the church

Focus group members were asked, "When Christian churches make changes in their teachings (for example, approving homosexuality or ordaining women), is it a matter of the Bible changing? God changing? People changing? Something else?"

A lifelong Episcopalian male attributed change in the church to people changing. And he saw that as a good thing. When the church moved to ordain women, he said, "Why not?" He summed up his position by saying, "I try to be more open."

A man with a Lutheran background expressed his delight in the fact that the church was willing to change. He said, "God doesn't change. The Bible doesn't change. People do. And changes are okay as long as they are done in a loving way."

A woman with a Roman Catholic background stated that she liked how the Episcopal Church allows changes. "People are allowed to change. That's why people stay in the Episcopal Church. Thinking outside the box is expected of you."

A man with a Roman Catholic background explained, "You develop a tolerance for struggle as an Episcopalian. The Episcopal Church has a place for reason. The Bible doesn't change, but there remains a tension between tradition, reason, and your beliefs."

A lifelong Episcopalian said he was ready to leave the church because of different changes. And yet what prevented him from leaving was an appreciation for "the church's strength in diversity of thought and procedure." By his own admission, his conservative beliefs make him "an isolated individual here." And yet his conservative beliefs are not threatened. He spoke of a conversation he had with his priest, when the priest assured him that as long as he accepted the basics of the faith, he could maintain his "ideas and interpretations and still be welcome here."

A lifelong Episcopalian teenager attributed change in the church to the fact that the church is becoming more like God. "God loves us all. It takes time for people to accept other people. God has already accepted other people as they are. The Episcopal Church is just ahead of its time in accepting all people."

A woman with a Roman Catholic background, who happened to attend the General Convention when the Episcopal Church approved the ordination of women, was in favor of changes in the church. She remarked that "people jump to conclusions about changes instead of trying to learn about changes and accept changes."

A woman with a Lutheran background said that the answer to the question was a "combination of 'people changing' and 'something else.' The hysterical fear of and prohibitions against women, or lepers, or people of color, homosexuals, or epileptics, or anyone different are not the same now as in biblical times. Modern societies have more knowledge and, therefore, less fear. That is the 'people changing' part. The 'something else' part is, perhaps, grace or something akin to it that allows space for expansion in our beliefs and practices without feeling like we are sacrificing the sacred."

Uniting the diversified

"If Episcopalians are diverse in their teaching and belief, what is it, in your opinion, that unites Episcopalians?"

A female responded, "In my opinion, there is no one thing that unites us as Episcopalians. We love our *Book of Common Prayer,* our hymnals, our traditions, our disregard for those traditions, the different flavors of our faith around the world, the encouragement to ponder Christ's message to discover what we are called to do in the world, knowing we will be welcomed wherever we visit."

A male explained, "The love of God unites Episcopalians. They all love God and the idea of taking care of our neighbor. The church has demonstrated love for others. Their heart is in the right place. They don't throw money, but themselves."

A male brought back the subject of change into the picture with his answer: "When there has been change in the church, there has always been a minority who can't accept change, so they leave. We're always ready to welcome back people who leave."

A female saw the liturgy being a uniting factor. "You can go anywhere in the country, and the liturgy is the same."

Strengths of the church

A question related to the previous one asked focus group members to explain what they saw as the strengths of the Episcopal Church. The following were listed as strengths:

"Acceptance."

"No accusations. The church supports you. You are right, no matter what you think. The church doesn't dwell on sin."

"One of the draws is the church relationship with the hierarchy. It is a matter of churches being given more responsibility, rather than following the dictates of the hierarchy."

"The strength of the church is the people in the individual churches. The people are the church."

"We are who we are. Our strength is in the people who find a home in the Episcopal Church."

The Book of Common Prayer

The final question asked the group members to describe the importance of *The Book of Common Prayer* in their worship and devotional life.

A woman who had been raised in the Methodist church said that it was the liturgy that drew her to the Episcopal Church as a teenager. She sees the liturgical part of *The Book of Common Prayer* as the most important part.

A lifelong Episcopalian teenager said that when he was given a copy of *The Book of Common Prayer* at his confirmation, it made him feel a part of the church.

A woman who had formerly been Lutheran said, "It is warm. It is comforting. It is poetry. It is wisdom. It gives voice to my soul in my prayer and worship."

Review: Members of an Episcopal Church speak freely about their faith and their church. The comments of the individuals illustrate the diversity of thought and opinion that the church embodies. Their worship life, especially the use of *The Book of Common Prayer,* is a unifying factor in their lives.

CONCLUSION

So what can one conclude about the Episcopal Church? Here is how one Episcopal parish asks and answers that question: "So is the Episcopal Church 'Conservative' or 'Liberal'? Again, the only possible answer is 'both,' or perhaps 'all.' Within ECUSA you will find individuals and churches inhabiting all points of the spectrum, theologically, liturgically, socially and politically. And, people being people, it's probably not a good idea to get too hung up on labels. One person may be very 'conservative' theologically and liturgically, but quite 'liberal' socially and politically. The reverse is also true. You can't really point to one person (or parish or diocese or province) and say 'that's what Episcopalians are like.' While this situation can cause a lot of tension, it can also result in great richness and diversity."[117]

The church and its members

The preceding paragraph and, for that matter, the preceding pages of this book highlight the differences between the questions "What does an Episcopalian believe?" and "What does the Episcopal Church believe?" Answering the former question can come about only by asking individual Episcopalians what they believe. Answering the latter question is possible by examining official church statements and teachings.

When one examines the Episcopal Church as a whole, one sees a church that

- teaches that salvation is God's doing through the redemptive work of his Son, Jesus Christ. Individuals hold to a variety of viewpoints, some of which (like denying Jesus' resurrection) take some outside the realm of Christendom. But the church's official position points to Jesus as the only way of salvation.

- administers the sacraments of Holy Communion and Holy Baptism. In regard to Holy Communion (Eucharist), the church finds common ground with Reformed churches in believing that Jesus' body and blood are only spiritually received. Once again, individual clergy and laity understand the Lord's presence in the sacrament in different ways.

- recognizes Scripture, tradition, and reason as the tools for guiding people in their lives of faith and Christian living. Scripture is seen as the first point of reference, but tradition and reason are close companions.

- values and encourages diversity in thought, belief, and practice. The attitude of thinking outside the box is illustrated by one Episcopal Church TV ad that ran in the San Francisco Bay Area in 2000 and 2003. It said: "Jesus died to take away your sins, not your mind. Whoever you are, the Episcopal Church welcomes you."

- cherishes liturgical practices. Practices vary from parish to parish, but the use of *The Book of Common Prayer* is what especially enables Episcopalians to maintain a common identity with one another.

- possesses and displays an ecumenical spirit. The church understands different levels of ecumenicity, with "full Communion" being at the top.

- actively engages itself in political and social issues. In the spirit of Anglican thinking, the church will often take both sides of an issue and then allow individual members to act as they feel led.

One of the church's biggest strengths, in its opinion, is that there is "room in the tent" for diverse thought and practice. After examining the church, one can only conclude that the canvas of the tent is stretching and tearing, and some of the tent pegs are being pulled out. Many Episcopalians see and hear the same things and are concerned.

Understanding individual Episcopalians

One understands a church by reading documents, periodicals, and other publications by the national church or local parishes. One understands the people who belong to churches by listening to them.

A confessional Lutheran who seeks to understand the beliefs of an Episcopalian does well not to make any assumptions. As has been shown repeatedly, the Episcopal Church is not a church whose faith and practice is bound together by confessional statements. Rather, it is a church in which people agree on a few items and then agree to disagree on many more items. For that reason, local parishes and individual members may represent a wide range of beliefs and opinions. Rather than making assumptions, those interested in understanding Episcopalians would do well to ask questions and then listen to the answers.

The answers that individual Episcopalians give to questions may reveal how much they follow Scripture, tradition, or reason. While it is good to meet people where they are in their answers, confessional Lutherans can do the most good by directing Episcopalians, or anyone else for that matter, to Scripture. It is finally in Scripture where we find truth, unchanging truth. It is finally through Scripture, God's Holy Word, that the Holy Spirit works to change hearts and minds and lives. Ultimately, Jesus' prayer for his first disciples is our prayer for others: "Sanctify them by the truth; your word is truth" (John 17:17).

Closing thoughts

This book's purpose is not to bash or embarrass the Episcopal Church. At the outset I stated that "it is my intent to use the information I gathered from all my research to paint an accurate picture of the contemporary Episcopal Church." My goal has been to give readers, especially confessional Lutherans, an idea of what the Episcopal Church—past and present—is all about. If this information helps you share the truth with an Episcopalian friend or relative, this goal has been reached.

ENDNOTES

[1] *Church Acts* (Buffalo, New York: Diocese of Western New York, January 2004), p. E.

[2] *Episcopal News Service*, July 14, 2004.

[3] http://www.episcopalchurch.org/eppn.htm.

[4] http://www.adherents.com/rel-usa.html#religions

[5] Philip Schaff, *History of the Christian Church*, Vol. 4 (Grand Rapids: Wm. B. Eerdmans Publishing Company, 1920), p. 42.

[6] http://www.goodshepherdkingwood.org/whatis.htm.

[7] Christopher L. Webber, *Welcome to the Episcopal Church: An Introduction to Its History, Faith, and Worship* (Harrisburg, Pennsylvania: Morehouse Publishing, 1999), p. 98.

[8] *The Book of Common Prayer: According to the Use of the Episcopal Church* (New York: Oxford University Press, 1990), p. 855.

[9] http://gc2003.episcopalchurch.org/documents/WO_RTW2_part3.pdf.

[10] *The Book of Common Prayer*, p. 856.

[11] Ibid., p. 856.

[12] Ibid., p. 510.

[13] Ibid., p. 855.

[14] Stephen Sykes and John Booty [eds.], *The Study of Anglicanism* (Philadelphia: SPCK/Fortress Press, 1988), p. 29.

[15] Ian T. Douglas, *An Imagined Conversation on the Lambeth Commission with the Rev. Ian T. Douglas, Ph.D.* (© Ian T. Douglas, September 28, 2004), p. 3. Used by permission of the author.

[16] http://www.episcopalchurch.org/3577_51048_ENG_HTM.htm.

[17] Douglas, *An Imagined Conversation*, p. 5.

[18] http://www.episcopalchurch.org/3577_41331_ENG_HTM.htm.

[19] http://www.episcopalchurch.org/3577_59116_ENG_HTM.htm.

[20] Douglas, *An Imagined Conversation*, p. 5.

[21] *The Lambeth Commission on Communion—The Windsor Report 2004* (London: The Anglican Communion Office, The Anglican Consultative Council, 2004), p. 44.

[22] http://www.episcopalchurch.org/1275_59050_ENG_HTM.htm?menu=undefined.

[23] *The Lambeth Commission*, p. 44.

[24] Webber, *Welcome to the Episcopal Church*, p. 28.

[25] Luther D. Reed, *The Lutheran Liturgy* (Philadelphia: Fortress Press, 1947), p. 130.

26 Frank C. Senn, *Christian Liturgy: Catholic and Evangelical* (Minneapolis: Fortress Press, 1997), p. 382.

27 Ibid, p. 552.

28 *The Book of Common Prayer*, p. 160.

29 *The Lutheran Hymnal* (St. Louis: Concordia Publishing House, 1941), p. 54.

30 Gary Baumler and Kermit Moldenhauer [eds.], *Christian Worship: Manual* (Milwaukee: Northwestern Publishing House, 1993), p. 385.

31 *The Book of Common Prayer*, p. 166.

32 *The Lutheran Hymnal*, p. 62.

33 Baumler and Moldenhauer [eds.], *Christian Worship: Manual*, p. 403.

34 Reed, *The Lutheran Liturgy*, p. 128.

35 http://www.southernvirginia.anglican.org/cross/sep03/acts1.htm.

36 http://www.southernvirginia.anglican.org/cross/sep03/acts1.htm.

37 Dennis R. Maynard, *Those Episkopols* (Greenville, South Carolina: Dionysus Publications, 1994), pp. 24,25.

38 http://www.stmichaels-issaquah.org/FAQs.htm.

39 F. Bente [ed.], *Concordia Triglotta* (St. Louis: Concordia Publishing House, 1921), p. 777.

40 *The Book of Common Prayer*, p. 853.

41 Ibid., pp. 526,538.

42 Ibid., pp. 849,850.

43 Personal Interview, October 6, 2004.

44 *The Book of Common Prayer*, p. 305.

45 Personal Interview, November 17, 2004.

46 Bente [ed.], *Triglotta*, p. 45.

47 http://www.goodshepherdkingwood.org/whatis.htm.

48 *The Book of Common Prayer*, p. 858.

49 http://www.stpat.net/baptism.html.

50 http://stmatts.thediocese.net/mattbap.htm.

51 http://www.christchurchplano.org/services/baptisms.html.

52 *The Book of Common Prayer*, pp. 859,860.

53 Personal Interview, November 17, 2004.

54 http://justus.anglican.org/resources/bcp/1549/Communion_1549.htm.

55 Reed, *The Lutheran Liturgy*, p. 136.

56 http://justus.anglican.org/resources/bcp/1552/Communion_1552.htm.

57 http://justus.anglican.org/resources/bcp/1789/Ordinal_Communion_1789.htm.

58 *The Book of Common Prayer*, p. 873.

59 Ibid., p. 859.

[60] Personal Interview, November 17, 2004.

[61] http://www.catholic.com/thisrock/1999/9906fea3.asp.

[62] http://www.etdiocese.net/st-elizabeth/about_the_episcopal_church.htm.

[63] http://www.stjohnscornwall.com/what.htm.

[64] Bente [ed.], *Triglotta*, p. 47.

[65] http://www.st-marks-cathedral.org/ St. Mark Episcopal Cathedral, Worship Bulletin, January 2, 2005.

[66] http://trinityepiscopal.tripod.com/ Trinity Episcopal Church, Sutter Creek, California.

[67] http://www.trinitymatawan.com/page/page/583773.htm.

[68] http://www.st-andrews-episcopal.org/uploads/ Bulletin%20[2004.06.13]%20Pentecost%202.pdf. St. Andrew Episcopal Church, Greenville, South Carolina, June 13, 2004.

[69] *This We Believe: a Statement of Belief of the Wisconsin Evangelical Lutheran Synod* (Milwaukee, Wisconsin: Northwestern Publishing House, 1999), pp. 28,29.

[70] *Theology and Practice of the Lord's Supper Part One: A Report of the Commission on Theology and Church Relations of The Lutheran Church—Missouri Synod,* May 1983, pp. 22,23.

[71] *The Book of Common Prayer,* p. 860.

[72] *The Lambeth Commission,* p. 16.

[73] Ibid., p. 73.

[74] Ibid., pp. 77,78.

[75] Ibid., p. 78.

[76] Ibid., p. 78.

[77] http://www.st-tims-church.org/Read/con2000.html.

[78] http://www.nhepiscopal.org/html/bishop.html.

[79] *The Lambeth Commission,* p. 80.

[80] Bente [ed.], *Triglotta*, pp. 639,641.

[81] David P. Kuske [ed.], *Luther's Catechism* (Milwaukee: Board for Parish Education, Wisconsin Evangelical Lutheran Synod, 1982), p. 8.

[82] http://www.episcopalchurch.org/1866_37993_ENG_Print.html.

[83] http://www.episcopalchurch.org/41685_37993_ENG_HTM.htm.

[84] http://www.episcopalarchives.org/cgi-bin/acts_new/acts_resolution-complete.pl?resolution=1994-A054.

[85] http://www.capeepiscopalchurch.org/beliefs.html.

[86] http://www.resurrectionbellevue.org/q-views.htm.

[87] http://www.stjvny.org/parishbooklets/bklt_faq.asp.

[88] http://www.stmartinsbylake.org/spiritualresources/ Pentecost22WhatweBelievevs.Whatweallow.htm.

[89] Bente [ed.], *Triglotta*, pp. 633,635.

[90] http://www.southernvirgina.anglican.org/cross/sep03/acts1.htm.

[91] http://www.saintgeorgeschurch.org/ec_episcopal.htm.

[92] http://www.stjohnsclearwater.org/quickstartinfo.asp.

[93] http://www.staugustineepiscopalchurch.org/about_episcopalians.htm.

[94] http://www.saint-timothys.org/faq.asp.

[95] Webber, *Welcome to the Episcopal Church*, p. 22.

[96] Ibid., pp. 85,86.

[97] Thomas B. Johnson, *The Similarities and Differences between Confessional Lutheranism and Anglicanism: A Paper for Partial Fulfillment of Ordination*, 1997, p. 21.

[98] http://www.episcopalchannel.com/tvspots.shtml.

[99] http://stnicholas-elkgrove.org/worship.html.

[100] Maynard, *Those Episkopols*, p. 26.

[101] *Merriam-Webster's New Collegiate Dictionary* (Springfield, Massachusetts: G. & C. Merriam Company, 1977), p. 1279.

[102] Ibid, p. 1279.

[103] Bente [ed.], *Triglotta*, p. 1095.

[104] http://ecusa.anglican.org/eir.htm.

[105] *The Book of Common Prayer*, p. 877.

[106] http://www.eden.edu/cuic/cuic.htm.

[107] http://gc2003.episcopalchurch.org/6947_9206_ENG_HTM.htm.

[108] http://gc2003.episcopalchurch.org/6947_10367_ENG_HTM.htm?menu=menu6994.

[109] Ibid.

[110] http://www.elca.org/ecumenical/Resources/CommentaryonCalledtoCommonMission2.pdf.

[111] http://gc2003.episcopalchurch.org/6947_10367_ENG_HTM.htm?menu=menu6994.

[112] *Episcopal News Service*, March 8, 2005.

[113] *This We Believe*, p. 28.

[114] Ibid., pp. 28,29.

[115] http://www.episcopalmn.org/Bishop_Sermon_StClements_112603.htm.

[116] http://www.episcopalmn.org/Bishop_Editorial_081003.htm.

[117] http://www.goodshepherdkingwood.org/whatis.htm.